Prais

# Rental Properties
## MADE SIMPLE

I have had the privilege of Shiral Torres' mentorship for the last thirteen years. When I met Shiral I owned no investment property, but with her guidance I became an investor who bought and sold sixteen investment properties. I can honestly say I could not have done it without her. This book is a golden nugget that you'll reference again and again as you build your real estate portfolio. Your small investment in *Rental Properties Made Simple* will be returned to you repeatedly by implementing only a few of Shiral's tips!

*- Leslie Crumley, President, Personal Finance Strategist,*
  *Structured Success, Inc.*

Every year people contact our office regarding investing in rental properties. Whether they are first-time novices or experienced investors, I am so glad that Shiral Torres has shared her experiences in the form of her account of the successes and pitfalls in real estate investing. It's my pleasure to direct our clients to this wonderful book knowing that Shiral has constructed her advice in a manner that will truly assist others in making their real estate decisions. And knowing Shiral's heart, helping others will be the greatest gift to her.

*- David Christiansen, CPA, Christiansen Russell & Christiansen, CPAs,*
  *Arcadia, California*

As an investment property owner I found Shiral Torres' book *Rental Properties Made Simple* valuable beyond imagination. With tips and tricks that even a seasoned property owner will find useful, the beauty of Shiral's philosophy on property management is its simplicity. If you're looking for uncomplicated ways to offset the traditional headaches associated with property management, look no further. This book is for you.

*- Stacy Dymalski, Real Estate Investor and author*

5/31/2020

To: April,

My fantastic Mary Kay
consultant. Dream and
you'll see it come to life.

Much Aloha,

Paul

# Rental Properties
## MADE SIMPLE

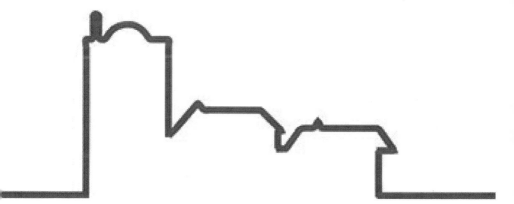

# Rental Properties

# MADE SIMPLE

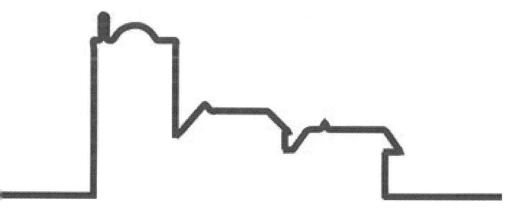

A no-nonsense,
straightforward guide
to managing your rental properties

by Shiral J. Torres

Published in the United States by
Simply Shiral

ISBN: 978-0-9995226-0-8

Library of Congress Control Number: 2017918957

Edited by: Stacy Dymalski, The Memoir Midwife™

Book cover and interior design by: Katie Mullaly, Surrogate Press™

Author photo by: Christopher O'Keefe, Attis Photography

To Jaime, Anita, and Jaime Jr.,
with you, my life has meaning.

In memory of Mom & Dad.
My rental property education started with you
and I am truly grateful.

and

Christina Long
for helping me turn my thoughts into reality.

# Table of Contents

# Introduction

Do you find yourself overwhelmed regretting you ever bought rental properties? Or are you new to this field and want to learn all you can before taking the plunge? Either way, after you read this book, you will be as happy as any landlord on rent collection day. How do I know? Because I've been right where you are now, and I know how to get to where you want to be in the real estate market.

Let me tell you my story of how I got started.

Nobody started further from the top than I did. I grew up in the "hood" of Los Angeles where drugs, alcohol, and gang violence were all around me. I was a good kid, got good grades, and had a supportive Hawaiian family. I was a tomboy, rode a dirt bike, helped my dad fix things, and I did needlework.

But when I was thirteen I met a boy, Jaime. We fell in love as all teenagers do, or think they do, and spent all our free time together. Did anyone ever talk to us about the birds and the bees? Nope. Which is why we got pregnant when we were both just sixteen years old. All you parents out there, PLEASE talk to your teenagers about the birds and the bees!

I won't go into how scared I was to tell my parents. (But of course, I did, I had to!) We decided I would continue to live at home with my family and Jaime would live with his. After giving birth to the most beautiful baby girl, I took a year off from high

school, returned in the fall, and Jaime left high school and found a job.

I was very lucky to have understanding parents who supported every decision I made. I finished high school a year after my graduating class, and when Jaime and I turned twenty-one we got married. Oh my gosh, what were we thinking? This is when finances became even more challenging because now we had to pay rent. Did I say rent? Yes rent, that lovely word property owners wait for every month (which I will talk about at length in Chapter Fourteen).

You can imagine the challenges a young couple faces raising a growing child and living on one (very small) income. I'm sure you all can visualize the difficulties. Fortunately I was (and still am) very good at managing a budget. Remember this word "budget" as it is one of the most important skills in this business. In fact, it's so important that I teach budgeting skills in two of my workshops. (For more information about my workshops visit my website at *www.simplyshiral.com.*)

Somehow Jaime and I managed to make ends meet, so I decided to pursue my dream to be a college graduate and enrolled at Los Angeles Valley College. Even with the additional challenges of being a college student, as well as giving birth to our second child, life seemed to get better. And after a couple of years I graduated from junior college and enrolled in California State University, Los Angeles. At this point my life was all about getting up early, getting the kids to school, taking the bus to college, picking the kids up after school, maintaining a home, helping with homework, cooking dinner, making lunches for the next day, then collapsing into bed, only to repeat it all over again the next day. You all know the

drill. It's all about consistency, which is a great tool to have when owning rental properties.

I finally finished college with a bachelor's degree in Sociology, a major I choose because I was a teenage mother and I wanted to work and help other teenage mothers. After I received my degree and went job hunting, I realized that all my education was in the field of substance abuse and alcohol addiction. I ended up accepting a job as an outpatient counselor at Asian American Drug Abuse Program, Inc. (AADAP), a substance abuse program in South Los Angeles.

Now both Jaime and I had good jobs. Things were going pretty well, as most households with two-income families. But of course, life has a way of keeping things interesting. Ready for my next challenge? Hold on to your seats because it's a big one. As I drove home from work one evening with my son in the car, the tire on the truck in front of us came off and lodged under my beautiful pink Volkswagen bug. We flipped upside down and slid down the 134 Freeway just before our exit on Buena Vista Street. Thank my lucky stars and all the gods and goddesses looking over us that my son got out of this with only a slight cut on his head.

But I wasn't so lucky.

I fractured my neck in four places, which led to a long and painful recovery. In the hospital the nurse told me I may not make it. (What? How dare she say that to any patient!) My doctor said I most likely would be paralyzed and never walk again. I was thirty-one years old.

But I would have none of their pessimistic nonsense. I said to all of them, "I am going to be just fine, because I've got kids to raise."

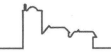 

True to my word, and much to the medical community's amazement, two weeks later I left the hospital in a wheelchair with a halo screwed into my skull. If you have not seen a halo before, it looks pretty devastating. But actually, it's just a cast for your neck.

I was determined to recover and resume a normal life. In six months I went from being in a wheelchair, to walking with a four-legged cane, to walking with a two-legged cane, to walking with a one-legged cane, to using no cane at all, until I was finally able to power walk all over Burbank, California. And today, by looking at me, you would never be able to tell that I was in such a horrific accident. I do have pain in my neck and shoulder areas due to not being able to have full range movement of my head. But other than that, I'm fine.

Fast forward to 1997, at the age of thirty-two, Jaime and I were lucky enough to buy our first home in a nice middle-class neighborhood. A year later I noticed that prices on duplexes and fourplexes were not much higher than that of our home. After running the numbers on rentals versus mortgages, and knowing how much rents were, I thought, *hmm…is this profit truly real?* I called our realtor and asked her, "If a mortgage payment for a fourplex is approximately fifteen hundred dollars and rents for a one bedroom is about six hundred fifty dollars, then that would mean after collecting rents on three out of four of the units in the fourplex, and paying all the expenses, there would be a profit, right?"

She said, "Yes, that's right."

"Then why isn't everyone investing in real estate?" I replied. "Why aren't *you* investing?"

"Most people have bad credit and would not qualify," she answered honestly.

This is where it all begins; credit history. While many of our friends and coworkers were doing cash-out refinances on their homes and then using the cash to go on expensive vacations or buy expensive cars, we decided to do a cash-out refinance on our primary home and use the funds to buy a fourplex. As long as rents from the fourplex would support the payment of the refinance and additional expenses (like taxes), but still have a profit, it was a sure deal for us.

A year later, as our fourplex value continued to rise, we did a cash-out refinance on that fourplex and used the funds to buy yet another fourplex. We started repeating this strategy until we accumulated many units not only in our neighborhood but also across the United States.

Through my entire life's journey (starting out as a teenage mother, attending college while raising two kids, recovering from a devastating car accident) did I know I was going to be an entrepreneur, own two businesses and numerous rental properties across the U.S.? Absolutely not! But there I was, the owner of multiple properties, with a lot to learn. Persistence is what I had then and what I still have today. Persistence is what you need to own and successfully operate rentals.

For example, I learned that taking care of properties means not only paying mortgages, but also finding the right property manager for my out-of-state properties, handyman, and tax accountant. You also need to keep all your real estate-related documents organized, and know how to deal with all different types of tenants and be prepared for just about anything. I learned early on that the only way I was going to be successful at investment real estate was to educate myself, and on many levels.

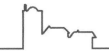

And that's exactly what I did.

Today managing our real estate investments is so easy I can do this in my sleep. And you can get there, too. That's why I wrote this book, for you, the potential property investor. I have taken all my experience, blood, sweat, and tears and put it all in this book so you can bypass the same learning curve mistakes I made along the way. I will guide you as a rental property owner, making you feel more confident in yourself and your decisions.

I firmly believe anyone can do this, but in my case, I didn't do it alone. Note that in this book when I say *we, us,* or *our,* I am referring to my husband Jaime and me. Even though I am responsible for most of the business and the property management, we make all the big decisions together. So those of you who have spouses or partners, get them involved with the decision making because in the end, it benefits both of you, and of course you always need a shoulder to cry on when you have a bad day.

So read on and enjoy the process. I wish you much happiness on your journey as a successful rental property owner, which hopefully with my help, will be less bumpy than mine was.

# Chapter One: Research

Most people don't like to do research, but it's one of the most important and valuable things you can do when starting a new venture. Unfortunately, we have to do the boring stuff just as much as the fun stuff to be successful. So I can't tell you enough how important it is to do your research.

At this point you may ask, "But what do I research?"

My answer is very simple – anything and everything! For example, if you need to find a course, realtor, property management company, or any of the other many professionals you'll rely on as a landlord, you start by searching the Internet, asking friends and neighbors for referrals, and checking out local advertisements. Find the outlet that meets your guidelines and qualifications for finding whatever it is you need. Keep looking until you find what you are looking for. This is research. Trust me, it is worth it!

Now think about your property investment goals. Is it to become rich? How do you define rich? We all have a different definition for the word. I define "being rich" as having supportive family and friends. Fortunately, I have that and so much more. Many people in the real estate field, however, define being rich as having lots of cash and properties. Sounds good, right? So how do we get all that cash and an abundance of properties?

To make cash flow using real estate, one needs to start out by buying a piece of property. Well, that seems pretty obvious, but how do you get cash to buy properties? Some options are:

- Apply for a bank loan.
- Use your home equity (if you already own a home) by doing a cash-out refinance. (Equity is the cash value of a property or business beyond any amount owed on it.)
- Save for the down payment (if doing a bank loan).
- Use an inheritance.
- Borrow money from friends or family.
- Liquidate stocks or investment portfolios.

Really, that's it. Either you have access to the cash or you don't. Once you have the cash, there are many strategies to buying properties. To find one that works for you, go back to your research; take a course, read a book, surf the Internet, talk to successful investors, there are so many options! I would say the easiest way to start is to take a course because then you can actually have a dialogue with your instructor about your real estate goals. But you have to be careful. There are many courses out there that lead you to believe you will easily gain financial riches without doing all the necessary work. BEWARE of those types of courses because they sell you the dream, but not the reality (or the responsibility). They teach strategies that most people won't be able to implement because their strategies are complicated, or they gloss over the hidden costs and legwork involved in buying and managing properties. I have paid thousands and thousands of dollars for some of these courses and after completing them, even me, the experienced investor, could not implement some of their strategies because they were either

too risky or just didn't make sense. So the first lesson I offer you is this: Don't make the same mistake I did by purchasing an investment course before researching it and before investing your time or money into any of them. Make sure whatever it is they suggest you do makes sense to YOU and is doable by YOU without getting in over your head with regard to time and money.

On that note, I would like to begin our real estate journey together by assuring you that I will be completely honest about my businesses successes and my failures. I will share with you what I know, and more importantly, what I don't know. I'll share my real-life stories and experiences in each chapter in a section I call *Story Time*. I use these stories to help illustrate the points I want to get across to you. It's important that you understand that I am not a realtor, an attorney, or an accountant, so everything I do and everything I write about is from real-life experiences (my stories). I'm just like YOU, except I've had a lot of successes and failures in real estate and property management, and I want to share all those valuable lessons with you so you can experience more successes and less failures than I did.

With that said, let's begin by talking about the most commonly used investment strategies for real estate.

## Strategy 1: Buy-And-Hold

Once you buy a property, you need to figure out how you'll use that property to earn money. The first strategy I'll discuss with you is called buy-and-hold. Personally, I'm a buy-and-hold gal, and I used this strategy to bring my husband and myself wealth. The buy-and-hold strategy is when you buy a piece of property, hold on to it for years and watch the equity grow. As the years go on, the equity in

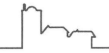 

your property rises, and that equity determines your wealth. From here you can control your destiny. When the time is right, you can either sell the property (and turn the equity into cash) or pull your equity out of your property and use the resulting cash to do whatever you want. For example, you can use the equity cash to buy another piece of property, pay off debt, or retire. Or you can keep the equity in your property and continue to watch it grow. Most often, the longer you keep your property, the more equity you'll have in it, and then the more cash you'll have when you finally decide to sell it.

Patience will get you ahead in the long run. In my opinion, buy-and-hold is one of the easiest and safest ways to go. This strategy is a good way to save for the future, because the equity can be used for anything from your child's college education to debt consolidation and more.

The pros and cons to the buy-and-hold strategy are as follows:

- Pro – You accumulate long-term wealth.
- Con – Your money (equity) is tied up until you sell the property.

## Flipping

Another common strategy in building wealth with real estate is flipping. Flipping is when you buy a piece of property, rehab it, and then resell quickly. It is not as profitable as one would think unless you keep within your budget, stay on top of all remodeling expenses, and know exactly what your outcome will be before you do the flip. This strategy is good for those who are familiar with rehabbing properties or have connections with people like

electricians, plumbers, carpenters, landscapers, and any contractor that you pay to do work on your properties.

The pros and cons to flipping are as follows:

- Pro – Fast cash.

- Con – Must have the time and money to complete this project.

- Con – Not understanding the tax implications of short-term capital gains.

That last bullet point above (short term capital gains) can really come back to bite you if you don't know what you're doing. If you plan on flipping, I highly suggest you talk to an accountant first. Flipping can have significant tax consequences because if you make too much of a profit in a short period of time, you may owe more taxes on that gain than you think. You don't want to flip a property, make a large amount of cash, spend that cash, but then find out months later at tax time that you owe capital gains tax to the IRS and your state. (I will define capital gains tax in greater detail in Chapter Four.)

## Airbnb

The most recent (and a very popular) strategy is listing your home or rental property under Airbnb. This strategy is for someone who already owns their own home. This is where a homeowner can do a short-term rental by renting out their home, bedroom, or rental house. Airbnb (*www.airbnb.com*) is an online marketplace that does all the work for you. This strategy became very popular during the housing crisis in 2008 when many owners had to foreclose or short

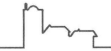
sale their properties. Many owners tried to rent out their homes or bedrooms as a way to earn income to save them from foreclosure.

If you already own a home, camper, guesthouse, or rental property this strategy can help you earn extra cash to save until you can purchase an additional property. The beauty of Airbnb is that it allows you to earn rental income without actually being a landlord.

The pros and cons for the Airbnb strategy are as follows:

- Pro – You can start this strategy with or without cash and earn money now.
- Con – You have to continually advertise for new tenants/houseguest.

## STORY TIME

A student in one of my workshops asked many questions about the real estate game. I noticed that the questions he asked were all about the fun part of the business (buying and making money), but he didn't want to learn the details involved in the step-by-step process that lead to buying property as a way to earn income. In other words, he focused on the dream and not the reality, very much like the unscrupulous courses I talked about at the beginning of this chapter.

Throughout the workshop, as I always do, I stressed the importance of doing research and processing the information before making any decisions. But then after my course was over, this student unfortunately jumped right into the flipping strategy without doing his research. He called me months later to tell me he

bought a house, fixed it up and sold it for a large profit. After I congratulated him, I asked him, "How much capital gains tax did you have to pay?"

He replied, "What is capital gains tax?"

"It is the tax you pay on the amount of the profit you made," I replied.

"I didn't know about this," he shot back.

"Did you do the research I taught you in the workshop?"

"No, because I knew the realtor who was selling the house," he said warily.

Long story short, after paying the capital gains tax on the home he sold, he realized he didn't make any money. He ended up owing the IRS money because when he created his budget before buying the house, he didn't include capital gains tax. I am sure if he decides to flip a property again, he will include capital gains tax in his budget. This is an example of a very expensive lesson for not doing the research. Please learn from his mistake.

## Summary

1. Beware of courses and programs that sound like get rich quick schemes.

2. Make sure you research any course, strategy, company, or consultant before you put your time and money into it.

3. Research the many strategies with regard to buying rental properties to find the one right for you.

4. Talk to your accountant before trying any new strategy or making a property purchase.

5. When working out the numbers before purchasing a piece of property, be sure to deduct all expenses before making the decision to buy. Just because a house looks good doesn't mean it cash-flows well.

# Chapter Two: Expectations

Expectations in a new venture are exciting because they are what motivates you to move forward. Like anything else, there are positive and negative expectations in the rental property business, however I will only cover the ones with which I am familiar or that I've heard about from other investors.

The most common expectation I hear from new investors is this: "I will earn lots of money from rental income." This is not always the case, especially in the beginning. New investors think, for example, if you own a rental property and the monthly rent is three thousand dollars, and the mortgage payment is eighteen hundred dollars, then you hit the jackpot because you just made a profit of twelve hundred dollars per month, or $14,400 per year.

Truthfully, it is not that simple. To illustrate why, let's break it down.

## Profits

In the model above, the landlord has not accounted for monthly expenses such as utility bills, gardening, pest control, and general maintenance that tenants expect and deserve. New landlords also often don't realize that you must set aside funds for miscellaneous expenses such as taxes, insurance, repairs and replacements, as well as large ticket items like a new roof, plumbing, electrical, and repainting the place every so often. Unfortunately, the expectation

of *I get to keep all the profits!* is very common. But if all these underlying expenses are not considered carefully, they can cause a new investor financial problems and possibly the loss of the investment property.

## Anybody Home?

Entering your rental property whenever you want is another common expectation that is completely unrealistic. Landlords must serve the tenant a *Notice to Enter* document before entering the unit. Most cities require at least a twenty-four-hour notice. New owners might object by saying, "But it's my house, so if I need to fix something, I'm just going in to fix it."

No. Big mistake! A tenant can sue a landlord if the landlord enters without proper written notice to the tenant. Check with your local landlord association, a landlord/tenant attorney, or the landlord/tenant rights department in your city and state. Even though you own the property, your tenants have rights as renters.

## Get Out!

Another misguided expectation is the landlord's ability to evict a tenant without reason. A new owner might say, "I don't like my tenants, so I am going to evict them." Before you even entertain the idea, once again please contact your local landlord association, a landlord/tenant attorney, or landlord tenant rights department in your city and state. In cities like Los Angeles, that have a Rent Stabilization Ordinance also known as *Rent Control*, there are specific guidelines landlords must follow when they evict a tenant. If your rental property falls under Rent Control trust me, eviction

is not that simple, even if the landlord is justified. I strongly encourage you to talk to a landlord/tenant attorney before evicting any tenant to make sure you don't break any laws, leading to costly fines and/or court fees on your part.

## STORY TIME

In 2008 my mom was diagnosed with Alzheimer's Disease. As I readjusted my life to take care of her, I knew this was going to be a long, difficult road, and that I would need help. My parents (both gone now) owned three houses in a row at the time in a neighborhood protected by Rent Control. Since I was taking care of my mother and needed help, my sister and I thought this would be a good time to give one of Mom's tenants a 60-day notice to vacate so my sister could move in two doors away from Mom. (Dad passed away in 1999 so Mom was all alone). At the time, because I didn't have any rentals in the Los Angeles area, I knew nothing about Rent Control. I called the Apartment Owners Association in Los Angeles County and the Rent Stabilization Department and to my surprise, I was informed that we would have to pay the tenant's relocation fees. I thought, *Okay...that sounds fair.* "How much will that be?" I asked.

I was shocked to find out that the fees added up to over eighteen thousand dollars! Obviously, there was no way we were going to pay that so we waited for the tenants to willingly move out on their own accord before my sister moved in.

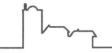

If you think this is unfair, you're not alone. The topic of evictions is one of many complaints a lot of landlords have with the Rent Control board. For more information about Rent Stabilization in Los Angeles visit *http://hcidla.lacity.org.*

## The Bottom Line

Overestimating the income line in your projected budget is the last misunderstood expectation I see most often by new landlords. It works like this: If you collect rent of one thousand dollars a month, for example, it's fair to assume that in a perfect world, your annual rental income would be twelve thousand dollars. On my budget spreadsheet, however, I personally decrease my projected annual rental income at least one hundred dollars every month per rental property, even if no repairs are scheduled or expected. I make this reduction to account for vacancies. With my rentals, it can take from two weeks to a month to get a vacant unit rent ready. So if I reduce my projected rental income, it won't affect my overall annual budget if I have a vacancy for one month. If I don't have a vacancy that year, then my annual income for that year is higher than projected, which is always a great thing!

Also remember to account separately for repairs, replacements, and cleaning fees that may be needed to get the unit rent ready. This is highly suggested because it is difficult to determine how much money it will take to make a unit rent ready. As you gain experience, it will be much easier to determine how much is needed. But for now, I would put away at least ten percent of each line item that relates to a vacancy (those line items being, for example, rent, utilities, repairs, cleaning, etc.).

And remember, when a tenant moves out, there are almost always some repairs needed, even if they are minor repairs like patching holes on the wall, painting, and carpet cleaning. If the tenant does damage to the unit beyond normal wear and tear, you can always take the repair cost from their security deposit. Check your local laws to see what fees you can deduct from a tenant's security deposit. I will speak further about security deposits in Chapter Seven.

## Summary

1. Cash flow is the balance after you deduct all line item expenses such as mortgage payment, tax, insurance, utilities, reserves, and maintenance from your rental income.

2. Be sure to learn about your local landlord laws before buying. Become a member of your local landlord association. (I will go over associations such as these in Chapter Thirteen.) There are landlord associations in every city and state.

3. Learn about The Rent Stabilization Ordinance, a.k.a. Rent Control, if this applies to your rental.

4. Create a projected budget that accounts for vacancies and vacancy-related expenses. If you have no vacancies in a year, then it's like getting a raise on your rental income!

# Chapter Three: Necessities

When you own and manage rental property, there are some things you can choose to do and some things you have to do. The things you have to do are necessities. However, I'm a firm believer in making some optional things necessities. Below are the things I do consistently, even though they aren't required. Why? Because doing things like keeping up with current laws, creating boundaries with tenants, and planning for the *What Ifs* in life helps me worry less, and thus allows me to enjoy life more.

## Keep Up On the Current Laws

It is absolutely a necessity to keep up with the current real estate and property rental laws. This is not a one-time thing when you purchase your property. It's ongoing because you never know which laws will change from one year to the next. State and federal governments modify and change real estate and property rental laws all the time. If you don't keep up with those laws, and you inadvertently break them, a judge is not going to excuse you because you didn't know the law. Ignorance of the law is never a defense. In fact, the judge may give you a larger fine because you simply should have known. If you jump into this game, then it's your responsibility to know the rules at all times.

## Plan for the "What Ifs"

It is an absolutely necessity to plan for the *What ifs*…better known as the unexpected. Owning rental properties is a little like having underage children. If you go on vacation, you need to find a sitter. It is the same for a rental property. If you go on vacation, you need to have someone in charge of your property while you are gone. *What if* something breaks down? You need a trusted person your tenants can call to take care of it. That person needs to have access to keys, service companies, money to pay for the service, and above all, access to you. That person also needs to know about the laws so that he or she does not inadvertently break them on your behalf. They need to know that a twenty-four-hour notice needs to be given to a tenant prior to entering their unit unless it is an emergency. Taking that responsibility even further, your stand-in needs to know what is considered an emergency in the first place.

You see how this can get serious pretty quickly?

Having a trusted person is crucial because you never know what's going to happen. *What if* you are sick and can't take care of these issues? *What if* you are at work and can't leave your job? *What if* you just can't be reached for whatever reason? These are things you must think about when owning rental properties

## Tenant Screening A.K.A. Credit Check

In my opinion, it is not only a necessity, but also a *must-do* to screen all potential tenants eighteen years and older before signing a rental agreement or lease with them. Even if the rental has been vacant for some time and you need the rental income, don't skip the tenant screening. If you do, you may later regret it.

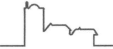
For your convenience, here are the Who, What, Where, and When aspects of running an effective tenant screening:

## Who: The Landlord (You)

To initiate a tenant screening, a landlord fills out the necessary forms to request the ability to screen tenants. Once approved by the credit bureaus the landlord can run a tenant screening on potential tenants. **Tip**: Do not run a tenant screening for anyone but a potential tenant. If you do, you are abusing the privilege and it may be illegal. You can complete a tenant screening online or go directly to your city's landlord association. The screening fee runs approximately seven dollars and up depending on the type of tenant screening you request.

## What: A Tenant Screening

A tenant screening allows you to review a potential tenant's credit history which helps you decide if the tenant will not only have the funds to pay the rent but also if the tenant is trustworthy in paying bills on time. Landlords can also run criminal background checks, look up civil judgments, view public records, check FICO scores, and more.

## Where: Your City in Which You Rent Your Property

Due to credit and identity fraud, most cities require landlords to qualify to run tenant screening. Landlords can apply easily through their local landlord association. Associations like Apartment Owners Association (AOA) and Apartment Association of the Greater Los Angeles Area (AAGLA) are required by state and federal law to

investigate and validate a landlord to make sure he or she is running a legitimate business and that the landlord has a need for a consumer credit profile. (Each state has their own requirements so check the landlord association in the state your property resides.)

## When: During the Application Process

You run a potential tenant's screening prior to accepting them as a tenant. Running it after they sign the rental agreements defeats the purpose of finding out if they pass your requirements. No matter how desperate you are to get a tenant into your property, do not let a tenant sign a lease or move in until you run a tenant screening first.

## STORY TIME

I met a landlord at a landlord meeting and he told me once he bypassed running a tenant screening because the tenant seemed nice. Plus, the landlord was anxious to rent out his newly remodeled house because he needed to recapture the expenses by finally collecting rent.

But just because a person is nice doesn't mean they pay their bills on time, are good housekeepers, or are good tenants.

A month later, when rent was due, the tenants paid their rent late. The following month the tenant said they didn't have the funds to pay the rent. This went on for five months before the owner gave the tenant a *Three-day Notice to Pay Rent or Move* notice. This landlord

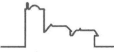

was very lucky that this rental did not fall under the Los Angeles Rent Stabilization Ordinance. If it had, he would have had a much more difficult time evicting these tenants. The owner started an eviction with an eviction attorney and the first time the tenant was served with the eviction notice, they moved out. The landlord only had to pay ninety-nine dollars because the tenant moved out right away. He was lucky. If the tenant hadn't moved out and the eviction went to court, the fees would have gone up thousands of dollars. And if the rental was in a rent stabilization city, the fees would have been even higher.

## Boundaries

Maintaining boundaries with tenants is my last unrequired necessity. Mom-and-pop owners, like me, sometimes have a difficult time with this, especially if you live next door to your rental. I like to maintain a friendly relationship with my tenants for many reasons, but mainly because I really am truly grateful to have them as tenants. After all, they are the ones paying my mortgage!

But if we, as landlords, don't maintain a professional relationship with our tenants, it becomes too easy for some tenants to take advantage of us. For example, if a tenant is late with the rent, you should immediately serve the tenant with a *Three-day Notice to Pay Rent or Move* document. This shows the tenant that you are a friendly landlord, but also a business owner. Believe me, if you don't give that *Three-day Notice to Pay Rent or Move* document to the tenant, they will most likely be late with the rent again and

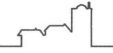

again because they know you don't enforce the rental agreement. Keep expectations clear and consistent right from the beginning.

## Summary

1. Keep up with the current real estate and property laws. They change constantly, so you can't rely on the laws that were current when you bought the property.

2. Plan for the *What ifs* in life.

3. Always, always, ALWAYS run a tenant screening on all potential tenants eighteen years and older.

4. Set boundaries. Be friendly with the tenants, but make sure you maintain a business relationship with them at all times.

# Chapter Four: Tax & Insurance

The most dreaded expenses of owning rental properties are taxes. Other than your mortgage payment, your property-related taxes are the largest expenses you'll pay. In this chapter, I will cover some of the taxes and insurances that are associated with rental properties, defining each in very easy-to-understand terms. I'll give you just enough information so that later you can check Google for the terms you need to learn in more detail.

And just to be safe, I suggest you talk to your accountant and insurance agent to find out what is best for your specific needs.

## Tax Bill

Property tax is levied on all real estate and is the most common tax all property owners must pay. It is an annual tax on each piece of property or land you own. A county assessor assesses your property to give it a fair market value, and then that value is taxed a certain percentage. That percentage is determined by the state in which the property exists. Because property tax percentages are state-based, the tax rate varies from state to state. Regardless, the amount of property tax you owe on a single piece of property is determined by multiplying the fair market value of the property by the current property tax rate.

## Supplemental Tax Bill

A supplemental tax bill is the difference between the last assessed value of your property and a new assessment. This is an additional tax you may or may not have the first year. To be safe, I suggest you assume that you WILL have to pay for a supplemental tax bill. So save for it.

On July 1, 1983, the California State law was changed to reassessing a property as of the first day of the month following an ownership change or completion of new construction. Therefore, if your property is in California, chances are, it's not a question of "if" you will get a supplemental tax bill after you purchase property, it is a matter of "when" will you get this bill, or bills because there may be two in addition to your annual property tax.

## STORY TIME

Back when my husband and I were in our early thirties, we were so excited to buy our first home and thrilled that we had enough cash for the down payment and other expenses that go along with buying a house. We were new to this game so I tried to learn everything I could to avoid any unforeseen costs. After completing some minor work on the house, we moved in. Since property tax and homeowner's insurance was included in our monthly mortgage payment all we had to do was pay our mortgage every month and we'd have all the mortgage expenses covered.

Or so I thought.

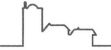

But about five months later, we received a supplemental tax bill. *What is this?*

I called my lender and she told me according to the Treasurer-Tax Collectors, when there is a change of ownership or a completion of new construction on a piece of real estate, then that property must be reappraised by the county assessor. This means the assessor's office sends out a supplemental assessment to the property owner (in this case my husband and me), which reflects the difference between the prior assessed value and the new assessment. (You'd think they'd get this done at the closing of escrow, but they usually don't, at least not in California.) The supplemental tax bill can be an increase or decrease in assessed value. For us, it was an increase and we had to pay that difference or there would be a penalty.

I thought I did all my homework before buying our home, but no one told me about this type of unexpected tax bill. Either our realtor, lender, or the title company should have mentioned that this was a possibility, but they didn't. In your case, make sure you know your property's assessed value, and the date of when the next assessment occurs, BEFORE you purchase the property. Specifically ask if or when you will receive a supplemental tax bill. If your property is in California, ask for an estimated supplemental tax bill at the closing of your escrow.

## Capital Gains Tax

Capital gain is the profit on the sale of an asset; it's the difference between your purchase price and sale price of that asset (in this case your property is the asset). One day you may want to sell your property. One way to help offset this tax is to keep accurate records on all the improvements you make on your property. In other words, keep your bookkeeping records and receipts that will prove that you did the improvements because they can be deducted from your gains dollar for dollar. Remember you only have to worry about this when you sell your property, but in order to do this you have to keep improvement records as they happen. In my workshop, Rental Properties Made Simple, I have a spreadsheet that you can use to keep track of your improvements. (For information on this and other workshops, check out my website at *www.simplyshiral.com*.)

## Other Taxes

Other taxes that may apply to you are corporate tax, business tax, and self-employment. I pay $32 a year in business tax per rental building and that adds up. That's why in my workshop I encourage people to save, save, save for unforeseen fees. To learn more about tax rates in your area visit *www.tax-rates.org*.

## Rental Property Insurance

Rental property insurance can have many names like rental dwelling policy, apartment policy, or investment property insurance. No matter what your insurance company calls it, an insurance policy

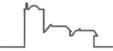

to protect your property is required before the closing of escrow. A policy for each property you own is required if a bank services your loan. The policy and premiums vary in each state. Most major insurance companies like State Farm, AAA, and Farmer Insurance have rental property insurance. I suggest calling your homeowners insurance or auto insurance company and ask about their rates. Most insurance companies give you huge discounts when you have multiple policies with them.

## Earthquake Insurance

Earthquake insurance is not included in your homeowners or rental property policy. It is a separate insurance that is purchased in addition to your current policy. In the past, rates were very high and the deductibles were outrageous. Compared to the $86,000 deductibles from the past, today there are many options to choose from with deductibles as low as $18,000 with a monthly payment of about $160, which is very affordable. It's pricey, but you should consider covering your property against earthquake damage, especially if you live in the western United States. The California Earthquake Authority, a.k.a. CEA, is one of the largest earthquake insurance companies. To learn more about earthquake insurance visit the CEA website at *www.earthquakeauthority.com.*

## Umbrella Policy

An umbrella policy is insurance for your insurance. This policy kicks in to pick up the slack when the main homeowner's insurance policy maxes out as a result of a claim or lawsuit. An umbrella policy is not required, but if you can afford such a policy, it provides

additional peace of mind. Why? Because if you are sued, for example, and your regular insurance policy covers only so much legal fees and liability (which can happen if you go to court), an umbrella policy takes over once your regular insurance policy hits its limit.

Umbrella policies are not required, but if you can afford this coverage, I highly recommend you get it.

## Summary

1. The rental property business has several tax bills that an owner is required to pay: annual tax bill, supplementary tax bill, and capital gains tax. It is important to learn about each one so you can set aside required funds for when they are due.

2. On July 1, 1983, California law was changed to reassess a property as of the first day of the month following an ownership change or completion of new construction. Therefore, you will receive a supplemental tax bill in addition to your annual property tax bill. Set aside funds to pay this.

3. Rental property insurance is another cost required by a rental property owner. Banks will not service your home loan if the rental property does not have rental property insurance.

4. Insurance companies offer other types of coverage, such as umbrella policies, that give you added security. These policies are not required, however I highly recommend them for peace of mind.

# Chapter Five: Asset Protection

What is an asset? For the purposes of our discussion, an asset is an item of ownership that can be converted into cash. For example, real estate, appliances, fixtures, and machinery (to name a few) are all things you can sell for cash. Because assets have value, you have to protect your assets from unexpected liabilities like lawsuits. So managing asset protection (in case of a *What if* scenario, for example) is something you might want to consider a necessity rather than an extra.

Unfortunately, we live in a time when anyone can sue anyone for any reason, even if the lawsuit is frivolous. Sometimes people or companies take unfair advantage of this, which is why it's best to protect yourself *and* your assets. No matter how much protection you have, however, you can still be sued. But it makes it more difficult for someone to win (and take your assets) if you prepare yourself for the worst-case scenario. I will talk about ways to lessen your chances of being sued in *Chapter Six: Liabilities.* In this chapter, however, I will cover different types of asset protection.

## Entities

An "entity" entails being or existence, especially when considered as distinct, independent, or self-contained.

There are five main types of Entities; C-corporation, S-corporation, 501(C)(3), Limited Liability Company (LLC), and

Partnership. Setting up a corporation to run your business is sometimes used as an asset protection plan. Plus, as a bonus, having your business function as a corporation can lighten your tax liability.

There are many reasons you would consider setting up a corporation, however a big reason is that a corporation can protect your assets and can provide tax benefits.

## STORY TIME

When I first started buying properties I enrolled in real estate investment courses. That's when I learned about asset protection. At the time, I did not have any type of asset protection, and when I realized how vulnerable my assets were, I freaked out. So, what did I do? I did what every naive new investor does; I bought into one of those programs that sets up a corporation for you. Was it expensive? Hell, yeah. Was it worth it? Well, let's look at the positives and negatives.

The obvious positive was that my personal assets were now protected. If someone decided to sue me, they can only go after the assets in my corporation but not the assets of the officers in the corporation, so there's one checkmark on the plus side. This made me feel secure so I could sleep at night. There's the second checkmark. Plus, having a corporation meant that the general public looked at my real estate endeavors as a real business, which made me appear more professional...three checkmarks!

Now let's look at the negatives, the biggest being it's very expensive to set up a corporation in California. Did

you hear me? EXPENSIVE. That's checkmark number one on the negative side, and it's a huge one. And then there's the extensive learning curve – I had to figure out my monthly and quarterly corporate duties to keep my corporation going, all of which was completely foreign to me...two checkmarks. After that I had to implement everything that is required to operate as a corporation, like owner's meetings, minutes, and K-1 forms, none of which is trivial...three checkmarks. Plus, in California there is an $800 minimum franchise tax annually to run a California corporation, whether the corporation makes a profit or not...four checkmarks! This means that even if your California corporation did not make any money, even if it *lost* money, you still owe the state a minimum of $800 in corporate tax. (This does not apply, however, in other states – just California. In fact, some states, like Florida and Nevada, don't even have state income tax.) Because of all these hidden corporate cost, you want to make sure that you earn enough annual income in the first place to justify incorporating your business no matter what state you live in.

The bottom line is this: corporations are a good way to protect your assets and lower your tax liabilities IF you have the energy and time to learn about them, implement that knowledge into your business, and stay on top of the monthly, quarterly, and annual paperwork. I will admit, it is different today (from when I started a corporation years ago) because now you can learn everything on the Internet and either create a

corporation on your own or find someone who can set it up for you for a reasonable fee. I suggest you do your due diligence before setting up your own corporation.

## Insurance Versus Entities

After our corporation discussion above, you may say to yourself, "Can't I just buy liability insurance to protect my assets?" The answer is yes. The most common types are personal and commercial umbrella liability policies, which I talked about in Chapter Four and then again in Chapter Six. And yes, buying an umbrella liability policy is much less expensive than starting an entity, so you need to talk to your accountant, insurance agent, and estate-planning attorney before you decide what's right for you.

When I first started my business, my dilemma was, paper or plastic, oops wrong book. My dilemma (when it came to protecting my assets) was do I create an entity or simply buy liability insurance? An attorney will tell you to create an entity and the insurance agent will tell you to buy the insurance. That just tells me that the attorney and the insurance agent are looking out for what's most profitable for them. (As you can see, I have trust issues.) My advice to you is learn all you can about both incorporation and liability insurance, and then with the help of trusted friends, family, and advisors make a decision that is best for your business. You just might decide to do both.

## Living Trust

A living trust is something I believe everyone should have. A living trust is a trust that you establish during your lifetime (i.e. while

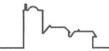
you're still living). You can put your assets (like your property) in your living trust, thus enabling you to control those assets before and after your death. Once you do pass on, your living trust keeps your family members out of probate court and prevents them from having to pay enormous death taxes and fees just to settle your estate. You can create a living trust by contacting an estate-planning attorney. Getting recommendations from family or friends is the best route to finding a good attorney.

## Summary

1. Entities and some types of insurance policies can provide asset protection so that you don't lose your real estate property (or other assets) in a lawsuit.

2. Do your research on entities versus liability insurance (to protect your assets) by talking to an accountant, insurance agent, and estate-planning attorney to decide what is best for your business.

3. Protect your assets (including your property) by putting them in a living trust. A living trust keeps your family members out of probate court after your death.

# Chapter Six: Liabilities

Liability is the one thing that most investors don't think about when they are all excited about closing a deal on a rental property. Sadly, most still don't think about it even after the closing – not until something happens. Is this an accurate statement: "Knowledge is power"? Most say yes. But I believe otherwise. I think *"Applied knowledge is power,"* because what value does knowledge have if you don't apply it?

In the rental property field liability means this: If anything goes wrong at, on, or with your rental property, you as the owner will most likely be responsible for it. When I say wrong, this can imply lots of things, from a person falling and injuring themselves to tenants bringing in bedbugs that spread throughout the building. In most cases, a landlord can and will be held responsible for almost everything that can go wrong at a rental property. And your liability chances increase if your property falls under the Rent Stabilization Ordinance.

Almost every landlord I know has been sued. But I don't let this frighten me because I have my *What if* plan in place. Anyone can sue anyone, but winning is another thing. Every decision I make, I try to look at it through the eyes of a judge, regardless of what anyone else says. After getting advice from at least three attorneys or professionals, I then make a decision on what I think a judge would say or do. I figure that if I do my routine inspections, follow

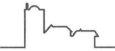 

all the laws, have a positive attitude, use updated forms, and have liability and commercial umbrella policies as addendums to our renter's policies, my odds of getting hit with a lawsuit are lower. However, I also know that even if I cross all my "T's" and dot all my "I's" I can still be hit with a lawsuit. But if that happens, at least I know that I am on top of things. Landlord liability is something that should not be taken lightly because if a tenant wins a lawsuit, it could be very costly to you.

One common type of property lawsuit is when a dog bites a person or another dog. After the following Story Time, I will give some examples that can help you stay away from common mistakes that open property owners up to unnecessary liability.

## STORY TIME

I met a mom-and-pop landlord who told me a story about when they were sued. They owned their rentals for many, many years, and as seasoned landlords they never had problems with any of their tenants having pets. So they agreed to let their new tenants bring in a dog.

One day, the tenants' dog bit one of the tenants' friends, so the friend sued the landlord. Now you would think since the tenants are the owners of the dog, and the friend is a friend of the tenants (and not the owner), the tenants would be liable for anything their dog does.

Wrong!

Even though you would think the tenants should be liable, according to the law, the landlord (as the owner of the property on which the dog bite occurred) may

be the responsible party. In this case, the owner was, and had to pay for medical bills related to the dog bite.

Sad, but true.

## No Pet Policy

How can we avoid a situation like the one above? That is a tricky question, because a landlord can do all the right things and *still* end up as the responsible party. That's why I always like to manage the *what if*. For example, at our multi-unit buildings, we just don't allow pets. With a multi-unit building, tenants live very closely together with no yard, therefore I think it is risky to allow tenants to have pets.

For our single-family rentals, we do allow pets, but under one condition. The tenant must have renters or liability insurance that includes pet insurance. We also require the tenant to put us (the landlords) and the property management company on the tenant's policy as "additional interest," so if the tenant stops paying their premiums, the insurance company will notify us. I also make sure it is stated in the *Rental/Lease Agreement* that the tenant must continue to have active renters/liability insurance that includes a pet policy.

## Smoke and Carbon Monoxide Detectors

Smoke and carbon monoxide detectors are a must in any rental property, both for the safety of your tenants and your property. The rules vary in every state so call your local fire department for updated smoke and carbon monoxide detector laws in your city.

Once you have your smoke and carbon monoxide detectors installed and functioning, check them regularly to ensure they

continuously work, and to make sure your tenant has not removed or disabled them. We all are guilty of disabling our own detectors at one time or another, specifically when they go off and we know there is no fire (and then forget to enable them again). We all have heard on the news about tragedies that happen due to faulty or missing smoke and/or carbon monoxide detectors. You definitely don't want to be held liable for something like that.

## Old, Torn Carpet

Replacing carpet is very expensive, especially if you have a tenant in the unit and all their things need to be removed in order to replace the carpet. Why would you want to replace old, worn carpet in a unit in which a tenant lives? Because torn carpet can be a tripping hazard, for which you as the landlord would be liable. And second, it is your responsibility to make sure your tenants live in a clean, safe, and well-maintained environment.

How do you determine if the tenant or you (the landlord) should pay for new carpet? If the damage to the carpet is caused by your tenant, find out what the average life of the carpet is by calling a carpet company, and then divide the cost of the carpet by that number and charge the tenant the amount that is left on the carpets life.

For example, let's say the carpet life span is eight years from the time it was installed, and the tenant has been living there five of those eight years, which means the carpet then has three more years of life left. If the tenant caused damage to the carpet and it all needs to be replaced, then the tenant is responsible for the remaining three years of the carpet's life. To determine the exact amount the tenant must kick in for carpet, use this formula; cost of carpet

divided by the carpet's life in years, times the amount of years the tenant is responsible for. To illustrate, let's say the cost to replace the carpet is $1,000. Divide $1,000 by eight years of carpet life, which equals $125 per year. Since the tenant is responsible for the remaining three years of carpet life, then the tenant is responsible for $125 times three years, which comes to $375.

If there is damage to a small section of the carpet, you would use the same formula for changing the small section of the carpet only.

In the past, I made it routine to replace carpet if it was in bad condition *before* a new tenant moves in. This avoids the hassle of the tenant moving everything out once they notice a dangerous tear. Or you can do what I have been doing since 2013; tear out the carpet and refinishing the beautiful hardwood floors under them. Hardwood floors are in fashion and they are easier and cheaper to maintain in the long run.

## Repair and Maintenance Technicians

If repairs and/or maintenance needs to be done on one of your rentals and your tenant is not home, I recommend you stay with the repair technician the entire time they're working, just to make sure nothing is taken or damaged. All you need is for your tenant to come home at the end of the day and then immediately call you to report something has been stolen. If you are there with the technician when the work is done, then you are a witness. Unfortunately, you need to be aware that a tenant may make a false claim anyway, but if you are with the technician the entire time, your chances of losing a lawsuit greatly decrease.

## Attitude is Everything

I strongly advise you to maintain a consistent, pleasant attitude with your tenants, no matter how mad they make you. (And they may make you REALLY mad sometimes.) Simply put, you are a human being and if you interact with tenants when you're upset, you may say something that you'll regret later. And "later" may come with a lawsuit. So be aware of your attitude whenever you interact with your tenants, whether it be in person, on the phone, or via a text.

## Rental/Lease Agreement

Routinely review (at least once a year) your *Rental/Lease Agreement* so you know what is on it and what needs to be added. You would be surprised by how many owners don't read their lease agreements. They have the attitude that if a boilerplate least agreement comes from a landlord association, then everything needed is already in it. However, some agreements don't include items that address things like bed bugs, pet insurance, move-in/move-out requirements, etc. If you need to add something to your agreement, then either find a form with the item already included or add an addendum to your agreement. If you do the latter, make sure your tenant signs the addendum, in addition to the agreement.

Lawsuits and court fees cost money regardless if you win or lose, and therefore can be very expensive either way. But if you do your due diligence your chances of being sued greatly decrease.

## Summary

1. Understand that you as a landlord may be responsible for some tenant claims even though it seems like you shouldn't be. Deal with those tenants and claims without getting overly emotional.

2. If you allow pets, require your tenants to get their own liability insurance that includes a pet policy, and insist that your name (as well as your property management company, if you have one) is on their policy as additional interest. That way, if they don't pay their insurance or it is cancelled, you will be notified.

3. Check smoke and carbon monoxide detectors at least twice a year to make sure they are functioning and enabled. In my Rental Properties Made Simple workshop, we review the maintenance spreadsheet I've created in class to help keep you organized and manage necessary and optional responsibilities.

4. Replace old, torn carpet to avoid harmful falls, for which you (the landlord) will be liable.

5. Stay with repair technicians if they must enter a tenant's home when the tenant is away.

6. Have a pleasant attitude with your tenants AT ALL TIMES. One rude remark can cost you down the road.

7. Read your rental or lease agreement at least once a year so you know if you need to make changes to it.

# Chapter Seven:
# Property Management

Property management in itself is a lot to write about and is one of my favorite topics. I am happy to share my experiences and the information you need to feel confident in this field. Throughout my journey as a rental property owner, my husband and I have always managed our local properties and hired property managers to take care of our out-of-state rental properties. In this chapter you will learn how to manage your own rental property and in Chapter Eight, you will learn how to hire and manage a property management company. In either case, however, I recommend attending your local landlord association workshops for continuing education, even if you use a property management company. I still attend these workshops on a regular basis.

By the end of Chapters Seven and Eight, you will feel confident in managing your own rental properties, as well as hiring and managing a property management company.

## Property Management By Owner

My husband and I have always managed our own local properties. The reason for this is very innocent; in the beginning, we just didn't have the money to hire anyone, even though we both had full-time jobs. My husband had a city job working with seniors and disabled people and I was a substance abuse counselor. Our careers didn't even come close to the nuances of the business world let alone real

estate. Let's face it, we we're new to this game and we had no clue what we were doing.

To educate myself, I went to monthly meetings offered by our local landlord association and began to learn about the world of real estate and property management. At times, I was excited by what I discovered, but on the other hand I often thought, *What the hell have we gotten ourselves into?* But no matter what I felt, I wasn't giving up because I knew, and still know, that rental properties are a great source of passive income that allows you to spend time on what matters most to you. **Tip**: if you start having feelings of doubt, take a deep breath and tell yourself "I won't give up before the miracle happens." Believe me, I am so grateful we didn't give up before our miracle happened, because now, every day, we live the dream of financial independence we had envisioned for ourselves.

## Rent Control

If you already own or are thinking about owning rental properties, find out if the area in which you wish to buy falls under a rent stabilization ordinance, a.k.a. rent control. I talked about rent control in Chapter Two, but it's worth mentioning it again. If your property is rent controlled, you must learn everything you can about the Rent Stabilization Ordinance so that you stay within the ordinance guidelines and not break any rules (which can be very costly). You don't want to find out later that you thought you were doing everything legal and then discover you violated something under the ordinance. The rent stabilization department has many free workshops related to its ordinance. I highly recommend you attend these free workshops. Let me repeat myself, I HIGHLY recommend you attend these workshops, rather than taking advise from someone

who may not be adequately informed (like a friend or neighbor who has or used to have rental properties). In this case, it's better to get the information you need directly from the source.

## Forms, Forms, Forms

There are lots of forms in the rental property business. Some of the forms you should keep on hand include *Application to Rent or Lease*, *Twenty-four-hour Notice of Intent to Enter*, and *Three-day Notice to Pay Rent or Move*. It is important to make sure all your forms are continuously updated. You can download the most current forms from your local landlord association, your state's housing websites, *www.evict123.com/free-forms*, or request one by contacting me at *www.simplyshiral.com*. When you fill out a form for a tenant, sign it and make a copy. Always remember to keep a copy of all forms and documents you give to a tenant for your records. I have added a list of forms that I use regularly. Ask your landlord association if any of these forms are needed in your area.

## Month-To-Month Versus Lease Agreement

Is your rental property business going to use a month-to-month rental agreement or a lease agreement? Let's explore both and you decide what is best for you. There is no right or wrong answer, you just need to look at the pros and cons of each and decide what is best for your business.

Month-to-month agreements are good for both tenant and owner because it gives both parties the option of ending the agreement in thirty days. I prefer month-to-month agreements for our local properties that we own and manage, because I want to be

able to end the agreement if I feel the tenant is not a good fit with the other tenants in the building. I also want the tenant to be able to move out if they are not comfortable living in our property. However, if I continue to have tenants who don't stay long, I would start using leases.

A lease agreement, on the other hand, is a contract that commits the renter to a specific time limit, and can be any number of months. Most owners use a one-year lease agreement. This means that the tenant and the owner cannot end the lease prior to the end of the time agreed upon. If the tenant decides to move prior to the end of the lease, the tenant will still be responsible for the rent until the end of the lease period. If the owner finds a tenant within that timeframe, the owner is then obligated to refund the remaining funds to the prior tenant. With a lease agreement, the guarantee of a tenant staying for the length of the lease is higher, which makes it easier to do a projected budget.

## Enter – Exit Checklist Form

I can't emphasize how important it is to complete an *Enter – Exit Checklist* form the day the tenant signs the rental or lease agreement. This is the number one reason landlords are sued. I go into detail about this subject in my Rental Property Made Simple workshop (for more information about my workshops go to *www.simplyshiral.com*). The *Enter – Exit Checklist* form is a record of the condition of the unit at the time the tenant moves in and when the tenant moves out. If you don't fill out this form when the tenant moves in, you will not be able to compare the condition of the unit to when the tenant moves out. Along with completing this form, it is very beneficial to take pictures of your property before

your tenants move in. In most cities, after a tenant moves out, the landlord has approximately twenty-one days to return the tenant's security deposit, along with an itemized statement that shows the expenses that were deducted from the security deposit.

## Security Deposit

This is a payment that a landlord requires a tenant to make BEFORE the tenant moves in. Typically, the landlord keeps the security deposit in a separate account for use if the tenant causes damage to the unit, property, or violates the lease. The security deposit is usually equivalent to one or two months' rent and paid when the tenant signs the rental or lease agreement. When the tenant moves out, the landlord uses these funds to repair any damages caused by the tenant. After that, the unused balance of the security deposit is then returned to the tenant. The tenant is responsible for all damage costs that exceed the amount of the security deposit. However, it can be hard to recoup damages after a tenant moves out, so you want to make sure you charge enough of a security deposit to cover the cost of fixing any potential damage, but not so much that it's too expensive for any tenant to move in.

## Keeping Rents Below Market Value

Market value is the average cost of rent for the neighborhood in which your rental property exists. My husband and I always keep our rents under market value. Why? Because if a tenant knows their rent is lower than their surrounding neighbors', they are more likely to stay. This is how we keep good renters. Constant tenant turnover is very costly. The cost can range as low as fifteen dollars an hour for

cleaning to thousands of dollars for the loss of rents while the unit is vacant. When tenants are happy, they stay. When good tenants stay, owners are happy. It's a win-win for everyone.

## Late Fees Versus Discounts

If rent is late, most owners charge a late fee after a three-day grace period according to the details outlined in the rental or lease agreement. For example, if the rent is due on the first day of the month, the late fee is applied on the fourth day of the month. I found when using this method, tenants eventually start paying their rent on the third day of the month instead of the first. **Tip**: Even though there is a grace period before a late fee is applied, the rent is still due on the first, therefore a *Three-day Notice to Pay Rent or Move* form should be delivered on the second day of the month.

Some owners use discounted rent instead of a late fee to encourage a tenant to pay rent on time. Using a discount is when you give a tenant a certain amount or percentage off their rent if it is paid on or before the first day the rent is due. I prefer using the discount option because I believe it is very important to maintain a positive relationship with tenants. Of course, every once in a while, there is a tenant who no matter what you do is still unhappy. We just need to accept this and not let their attitude affect us. Knowing that there are tenants like this, I always try to run my business with a positive attitude. I believe if a tenant is late with their rent and I give them a *Three-day Notice to Pay Rent or Move* form, the tenant will be upset with me, even though it is not my fault.

On the flip side, if I give the tenant a discount for paying on time, but then they are late, I can sincerely say to the tenant, "I am so sorry you won't get your discount." In most cases, the tenant is

not going to blame the landlord because the tenant feels grateful to have the discount when he or she DOES pay the rent on time.

## STORY TIME

When we had our first tenant give us a thirty-day notice to move, I reviewed the documents for that unit. This tenant was living in the unit prior to us owning it and the previous owner did not use an *Enter – Exit Checklist* form so I had nothing with which to compare his move out damages. Unfortunately, the tenant left his unit completely dirty and filled with so many of his things that I can't even write about it because I don't have the energy to relive it again. I assumed the unit was clean when he moved in so I charged him for the cleaning and repairs that were needed to get this unit rent ready. The tenant failed to send us the amount owed to us. I called an attorney and he said that because we did not have an *Enter – Exit Checklist* form there was a high chance that we would not win a small claims case. After learning the cost to take him to court and the high chance that we would not win the case, we decided to not proceed in recovering the damages. After this experience, we made sure we used an *Enter – Exit Checklist* form for every tenant.

## List of Forms

You can download the forms below in their most current versions from your local landlord association, your state's housing websites, *www.evict123.com/free-forms*, or by contacting me at *www.simplyshiral.com.*

1. Application to Rent or Lease
2. Deposit Receipt to Rent or Lease
3. Deposit Receipt and Offer to Rent or Lease
4. Rental Agreement
5. 30-Day Notice to Change Terms
6. 60-Day Notice to Change Terms
7. 3-Day Notice to Pay Rent or Move
8. 3-Day Notice to Cure Violation
9. 30-Day Notice to Move Out
10. 60-Day Notice to Move Out
11. 90-Day Notice to Move Out
12. Receipt of Residents 30-Day Notice to Move
13. House Rules
14. Addendum to Rental Agreement for Additional Tenant
15. Co-Signer Agreement
16. Pet Agreement
17. Service Animal Agreement
18. Roommate Agreement
19. 24-Hour Notice of Intent to Enter
20. Enter-Exit Checklist
21. Resident's Maintenance Service Request
22. Security Deposit Refund
23. Lead Based Paint Disclosure
24. Walk Through Process

25. Notice to Rent Application

26. Tenant Move Out Report

27. Notice of Belief of Abandonment

28. Satellite Dish Addendum

29. Receipt of Application Fee

30. Bed Bug Addendum

31. Information About Bed Bugs

32. Smoke-free Addendum

33. Protect Your Family from Lead in Your Home Pamphlet

## Summary

1. Find out if your rental is in an area that has a Rent Stabilization Ordinance, a.k.a. Rent Control.

2. Get updated forms from your local landlord association and when using these forms make signed copies for you and your tenant.

3. Decide whether you are going to use a lease or month-to-month agreement.

4. Use an *Enter – Exit Checklist* form for all tenants when signing a new rental agreement.

5. Charge all your tenants a security deposit.

6. Be aware of the market value of rents in your area.

7. Decide what is good for your business; giving tenants a discount for paying rent on time or imposing a fee if they are late with rent.

# Chapter Eight:
## Rental Property Managed by a Management Company

Some people are just not good at managing and if you are one of those people, it is better to hire a property manager. It is also better for those of you who own out-of-state properties to hire a property management company because you probably don't know all the landlord laws that pertain to your rental property area. Through personal experience, I can safely say that in most cases, it's safer to hire a property management company rather than a local person who just knows the house or the area. A property management company will keep up with current laws and use updated forms because that's their job. When dealing with out-of-state properties it is much easier for an owner to employ a property management company. When all goes as it should, the company you hire will do all the work, and the only time you hear from them is when they send you the monthly statement and rent check. They will also contact you when your tenant moves out or for repair costs that exceed an agreed upon amount, typically around $300. A property management company's fees are usually eight to ten percent of the monthly rent, which is a small price to pay for peace of mind.

### Hiring a Property Manager

I have learned the hard way, as I will explain in this chapter's *Story Time*, how important it is to interview property management companies before hiring one. All companies are not the same and

I want to hire one that not only meets my expectations, but also employs people with whom I feel comfortable. It is very much the same as hiring a staff member. I have a list of questions I ask when I interview a property management company, and I've included that list at the end of this chapter. To make it easy for you, here are the key questions I ask up front:

1. How soon is the callback time when the owner calls the management company or when the tenant calls the management company?

2. How do you handle emergencies?

3. What is your vacancy rate and how long does it take for you to rent a unit?

## STORY TIME

When we bought our beautiful house in Texas, and after interviewing property management companies, we decided to hire a small business property management company to manage our rental. The owner was fantastic and in my opinion, ranks on the top five on my list of best property managers. She managed our rental for many years until she passed away. After she passed away, her daughter continued to run the company. Since she worked for her mother as a property manager, I didn't even question her abilities.

About a year later, I noticed that she was not returning my calls as her mother did. Then she started sending my property management statements randomly instead of monthly. I questioned her and she gave me

excuses that seemed legitimate at the time. A month later, she told me that my tenant moved out and she was in search of a new tenant. I continued to keep in touch with her as the house sat vacant for at least five months. After continuing to put pressure on her, knowing that there has never been any problems filling a vacancy for this house, she finally found a tenant.

After a couple of months, I started having a gut feeling that something was going on, so I called the tenant. The tenant informed me that my property manager coerced her to pay rent weeks before it was due. I was embarrassed and shocked. I also found out that my tenant moved in three months prior to the move-in date that my property manager stated on the rental agreement.

After insisting that my manager tell me the truth and showing her that I had proof that she forged a fake rental agreement, she admitted that she lied and that the tenants move-in date was three months prior to the move-in date she had on the rental agreement. I immediately ended my contract with this property manager and found another one. I told my tenant to stop all contact with this manager and to not give her any rent. I am not going to write about what I did after I ended my agreement with this property manager except to say that I did take legal action.

The moral of this story is to make sure your property manager sends you not only the tenant's rental agreement but also a copy of their identification so you

can compare the signatures on the rental agreement with their identification card. I now have a management company managing this rental that falls on one of the top five best property managers on my list.

## Property Management Contract

You as the property owner must have a contract with any property management company you choose. If the company does not use a contract between owner and manager, and also a contract with manager and tenant, find another company. Believe me, there are many companies that don't use contracts and if you hire one, you will put yourself in a position for trouble. The contract between owner and the property management company should, at the very least, include:

1. The property management company's name, address, and phone number.

2. Date the contract begins and ends, with a discussion about renewal.

3. All fees charged by company, paid by owner, and paid by tenant.

4. Date when monthly statements and rent will be sent out and how they will be delivered (email versus snail mail).

5. Date and signatures by property management company, owner, tenant, and any others involved.

6. A copy of all rental agreements for your records.

7. The direct number and after hour phone numbers of the management company.

In addition, make sure the management company requires a security deposit from the tenant. And if or when problems with your unit occur, ask the property management company to call you before any repairs over three hundred dollars are done, and that you wish to receive receipts for all maintenance and repairs. And finally, make sure the property management company immediately informs you when a tenant leaves or gives a notice to move.

## Summary

1. If you don't have good management or people skills, a property management company is a better option for you.

2. Keep in mind that property management companies do things systematically, but a Mom-and-Pop owner (that would be you) can be more relaxed about things. Pick the option that is right for you and your business.

3. If going the property management route, interview property management companies to find one that works best with your business.

4. Review the management company's contract before signing it.

| Property Management Questions | |
| --- | --- |
| **Property Management Companies** | |
| Company Name | |
| Contact Person | |
| Do you have a Website? | |
| What is your Management Fee? | |
| Do you have a Leasing Fee? | |
| Lease Renewal Fee? | |
| Who receives late fee? | |
| Length of lease between Owners Agreement with Property Management Company | |
| Length of Tenants Lease | |
| How much do you charge for Security Deposit and where is it held? | |
| Do you have Direct Deposit? | |
| What is the Managers response time to owner? | |
| What is the Managers response time to tenant? | |
| Who does repairs? | |
| Are there Inspection Fees | |
| Does Manager own any rentals properties? | |
| How long has this company been in business? | |
| How do you handle emergencies? | |
| What is your vacancy rate and how long does it take to get a new tenant? | |
| | |
| Comments | |

# Chapter Nine: Organization

*For every minute spent organizing, an hour is earned.*
Benjamin Franklin

Most people think I'm organized. Actually, I'm obsessed with being organized. It's not only helpful to know where everything is, but it also gives me more time to do the things I love to do, like needlework, baking, volunteer work with Alzheimer's Association and National Alliance on Mental Illness, and most of all spending time with my family and friends. In this chapter I will cover simple ways to organize everything in your rental property business from creating an operations manual to storing documents.

## Operations Manual

Creating an operations manual may sound over-the-top, but it will be very useful if you ever decide to hire an employee or have a family member help you, especially since you can't always be around to train them. Creating an operations manual is a simple task if you take it slowly and develop it a little bit at a time.

Start by googling "Operations Manual" to get ideas on which template works best for you or your business. Then either download a free template to start with or create your own based on one of the templates you find. For me, I googled "sample owner's manuals" and the results of my search gave me great ideas on how I wanted my own operations manual for my rental property business

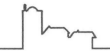

to look. Keep in mind, your operations manual doesn't need to be fancy or complicated, you just want someone to be able to open it up and understand the step-by-step process of what you do in your business.

Below is a simple step-by-step process to help you get started in creating your own operations manual for your business.

1.  Since a manual is a group of specific operational procedures, make a list of each task you plan to cover in the manual and then turn that list into an outline. This outline will act as your guide to ensure you do not leave out any of your property management tasks as you create your manual.

2.  Write an Introduction in which you speak to the people who will use this manual; these might be your family, employees, friends who pitch in, or anyone you can think of that might take over if you are not available. In your introduction make it clear which business this manual is for by including your business name, address, phone number, tax ID, and any other pertinent information that someone would need to know before they get into to the nuts and bolts of your business. Something like this:

    This operations manual provides important organizational information as well as operations procedures for *ADD YOUR BUSINESS NAME HERE*.

3.  Next, the most efficient way to complete this manual is to deal with your operational tasks one step at a time. Write down the details of each step, being clear and concise. Provide enough detail so that anyone can follow

the instructions in this step, but don't add unnecessary information that might be confusing.

4. After you've completed writing down everything for this task (as a step in your manual) give it to someone who can proofread for content and writing errors, preferably a reader who may actually have to use your manual someday. Your reviewers can give you valuable feedback especially if there are steps in your task they don't understand. NOTE: You may have different people review the different tasks/steps in your operations manual, or if you want, have the same person to review all the steps, you can wait until you've completed the manual before handing it off for review.

5. After your review copy comes back, refine the step(s) based on the feedback you receive. You may need to rewrite, edit, or add to some of your instructions. If so, don't look at this as a failure or disappointment, but rather as an opportunity to make your manual even better than it would've been.

6. Write the next task in your manual and then repeat Steps 3 to 5 above for each task (if you haven't done so already).

7. Compile all of the outlined tasks into a binder or bound manual. Include a cover sheet with the name of the manual, a table of contents, and your Introduction.

8. Make copies and distribute to employees, family members, and helpers. Encourage regular, ongoing feedback, and update when necessary.

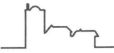 

If these steps seem a bit overwhelming to you, feel free to contact me for help at *www.simplyshiral.com* or email me at *shiral@simplyshiral.com* so we can work together to address your needs. Getting your operations manual right is vital to a successful property management business.

## STORY TIME

Creating an operations manual didn't come to mind, even after years into my business. Once you start your business there is so much you learn as you go along. I remember the day I realized I needed an operations manual. I always wanted at least one of my kids to learn about our business just in case something happened to me, because then I'd have someone who could take over, at least temporarily. However, I don't expect my children to permanently take over the family business. I want them to live their own lives and reach their own goals as they wish, and not feel obligated to take on their parents' rental property business if they are not interested in it.

That all said, about sixteen years after we bought our first rental, our son started taking an interest in our business and wanted to learn more. I asked him if he would like to work for me part time as my property management assistant. Lucky me, he replied, "Yes."

Once he started, he took notes every time I trained him on how to do a new task. Then I noticed that whenever he had to do a task, he referred to his step-by-step notes. That's when the light bulb in my head went on. *We can use his notes to create an operations manual,*

*so that we have instructions for all our business tasks in one place.*

If I hadn't hired my son, I probably would have never thought about creating an operations manual.

## Storing Documents

I know it sounds Old School, but I store all my documents as hard copies in a binder, as well as electronically on a flash drive and an external hard drive. (You could also use Google Drive, or the Cloud.) I do this as a double and triple backup of all my important paperwork, including tax returns, rental agreements, completed tenant forms, bank statements, mortgage documents, and anything I might need for any type of audit.

## Binders

Even though I do everything on the computer and have electronic backups, I still have hard copies in binders. I feel much more secure knowing that I have everything at a quick glance without having to turn on my computer. I have tons of binders, including a binder for each and every piece of property we own. I offer simple and low-cost workshops that teach students how to manage their properties, which includes a binder and my organizing system. For more information about my workshops, visit my website at *www.simplyshiral.com.*

## Flash Drives and External Hard Drives

I back up all my files and documents on a flash drive and an external hard drive just in case my computer crashes. I would suggest

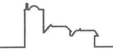 

you use some sort of backup for your documents, too. I buy my flash drives in sets of ten through Amazon.com, as Amazon has the lowest cost for flash drives that I've found online.

## Bank Accounts

No matter how you approach it, owning rental properties is a business. I don't want to freak anyone out with the word "business," but that word is used to help distinguish between personal income and expenses and rental income and expenses. Most of us have a personal bank account and a credit card. Whether you have one or many rental properties, it is much cleaner to have a separate bank account for your business to avoid comingling the funds between personal income and expenses and business income and expenses.

To open a business account, you will need to have some type of entity like a corporation, LLC, or DBA. If you don't have any of these, just open a regular personal checking account to use for your rental properties only. If you would rather open a business checking account, you will need to open one of the entities stated above. Getting a DBA (a.k.a. Doing Business As) is the simplest and most inexpensive way to open a business checking account. To establish your business as a DBA, go to the website of your county registrar-recorder/county clerk office and type in DBA or fictitious business name in the search box. The process is different in every state so follow your state's guidelines. Once you receive your certified copy of your DBA from your county recorder's office, you are ready to go to the bank and open your new business account. I know it seems like a lot of work just to open a business bank account but trust me, when it is time to do your dreaded annual tax returns, you will thank me for suggesting that you open one.

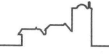

**TIP**: Many banks offer a free savings account with a new checking account. I would advise you to use this account to store your tenants' security deposits. This will help with the temptation of using the funds. I have talked to many property owners who have admitted that they use the security deposits and struggle when a tenant moves out and they need the funds to do repairs.

## Forms

Keep all your forms (blank and completed copies) in a file on your computer and in a binder so you have them right at your fingertips when needed. Most landlord associations provide the forms you need at no charge. Regardless, keeping a blank copy of your forms on file is handy when you need to access one quickly.

## Summary

1. Create an outline for your business operations manual and fill it in as you complete each task.

2. Store your documents in a binder, flash drive, and external hard drive, on Google Drive, or the Cloud.

3. Use binders to help you stay organized. You will be grateful you did if your computer fails you.

4. Back up your work in multiple ways. Don't rely on just one type of electronic backup system.

5. Open a separate bank account to use for your rental business only.

6. Download and print common forms so you have them at your fingertips.

# Chapter Ten: Property Upkeep

Maintaining rental properties is very similar to maintaining your own home. You keep it clean, fix things when they break, and replace items when they get old. The overall look of a rental unit is what appeals to tenants. If the rental is clean, maintained, and in good condition, the owner can rent it at a higher price. This chapter covers proper maintenance and upkeep of your rental unit so you can attract the best tenants possible and charge the rental rate you desire.

## Repairs and Maintenance

When you get that call from a tenant that something either broke, needs a general repair, or is scheduled for maintenance, make sure you and the tenant communicate about the work that needs to be done by using a *Tenant Maintenance & Repair Request* (a copy of this form is at the end of this chapter). If this request process is not stated in your rental agreements, you can always add it by adding an addendum and sending the tenant a copy. The addendum should state that you are adding a new policy that now requires all tenants to fill out a *Tenant Maintenance & Repair Request* if they wish any repairs or maintenance to be done. Also, add to the addendum that in case of an emergency (for example, fire, flood, structural damage, etc.), the tenants are required to call you immediately, but still send in the request form (later) to schedule repair of the damage.

If your tenant is new to this process, you will need to train them to use it. This is how I trained my tenants. When a tenant calls me for a repair, I tell them I will send out a technician, but then ask if they can fill out and send me a *Tenant Maintenance & Repair Request* form. As I continued making these requests every time I got a call for a repair, my tenants eventually turned in the request forms automatically without me asking them to do so.

Some benefits of using this form are:

1.  You have all repair requests and completed work for each unit on file.

2.  If you are ever taken to court for negligence, you have these forms to prove that you have a policy in place for repairs and maintenance.

**TIP**: I suggest not allowing tenants to do repairs or maintenance themselves in return for a reduction in their rent. This can cause too many problems and most likely the work will not be professionally done, which means it probably won't be correct or up-to-code. Plus, the tenant may overcharge you, and the discount on rent will be difficult to use as a deduction on your income taxes. Because how can you justify the expense when it was just a trade? It just makes everything more complicated trading rent for services, especially with regard to your bookkeeping, so please don't do it!

## Inspections

Typically, inspections on your property are done monthly, quarterly, or annually depending on what needs to be inspected and what kind of condition your property is in. You may want to drive by your rental once a month to see how it looks visually from the outside. If the yard looks neglected, it's a safe bet the tenants are

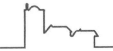

probably not keeping up the inside as well. For example, you may want to have quarterly inspections if you notice your tenant has lots of trash that is not in or near the trash cans. At the very least, I would suggest doing an annual inspection of the inside and outside of your rental to check things like steps and walkways, smoke detectors, carbon monoxide detectors, pipes, and overall appearance of the unit. Send the tenants a *Twenty-Four-Hour Notice of Intent to Enter* form and do a quick, yet thorough, inspection.

When you go to the unit to do the inspection, bring a clipboard and paper so you can write down everything that needs to be done. When you schedule repairs, send the tenant another *Twenty-Four-Hour Notice of Intent to Enter* with the date and time you will be back to complete the work. Know that in most cases, during an inspection the tenant will take this opportunity to ask you for things such as, "Can you put in a new faucet because this one is outdated? Can you take out the carpet and put in hardwood floors? Can I have marble countertops in the kitchen?"

Don't get caught off guard, be prepared with your answers so you don't inadvertently promise things you can't afford. I usually say something like this, "I will add that to our request list and in the future, if the budget allows, I will let you know if we can do it." If I know it will never be a possibility I simply say, "I'm sorry, it is not in our budget at this time to do any upgrades on items that still function well. This is how we are able to keep the rent low for you."

They will most often agree with you.

## Handyman

A good loyal, honest, and reliable handyman is hard to find. When and if you find one, cherish him or her, because this person is a key player in your business. Having a good handyman makes life

simpler for you to keep up with the repairs and maintenance of your rental properties.

## STORY TIME

When we bought our first home, we couldn't move in until we painted the living room and the kitchen, so I made appointments for estimates from three different companies. On the day I scheduled them to come look at our house, they came one after the other and said they would get back to me with their figures. Not knowing what the rate was for painting, because we were always renters and this was our first home, I had no idea what painting would cost.

The next day Company One gave me an estimate of $4,500. Company Two gave me an estimate of $5,100. Company Three gave me an estimate that I could not understand because Peter, the painter, had a thick Korean accent. I thought he said $350, but that couldn't be right, because the other estimates were in the thousands, so I asked, "Do you mean three-thousand-fifty dollars?"

He replied, "No, three fifty dollars."

"I'm sorry," I said, "I am having a difficult time understanding you because it sounds like you are saying three-hundred-fifty-dollars."

"Yes! That's right!" he answered.

"Are you sure your estimate is three-hundred-fifty dollars because everyone has quoted me over three-thousand dollars."

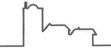
"Too expense, too expense, they charge too much, not right," he assured me.

I said, "Great! When can you start?"

While he was painting our family room, we learned that he was also a great handyman. When we bought our first small apartment building, Peter became our go-to handyman. I remember years ago Peter called me one day and said, "I charge you too much. I come give money back tomorrow." I had no idea what he was talking about because his estimates were always so low that sometimes I would add extra to his payment. Peter knew the inside and outside of all our properties better than we did, that's how good he was and still is.

I will never forget that day in 2006 when we met Peter Paik, the Korean painter who changed our lives forever. Peter is that needle in a haystack. He is not only our handyman, we consider him a part of our family. We know when Peter decides to retire we will never be able to find another Peter again.

But while he is still here, we are grateful and appreciate him for everything he has done for us.

## Vendor List vs. Preferred Vendor List

Having a vendor list saves you time and money when you get that unexpected call from your tenant that an emergency repair needs to be done. Having a vendor list in place also saves you time searching for a vendor when disaster strikes. Being a prepared landlord makes for a happy tenant. And remember, a happy tenant is a tenant that stays.

Before I give you the steps on how to build your vendor and preferred vendor list (sample forms are at the end of this chapter), you first need to learn how to find a reasonable and honest vendor. Since plumbing is always the number one issue, let's build a plumbing vendor list to illustrate this process. Here are the steps to finding a good plumber (which can also be applied to any vendor or contractor):

1. Write down a list of questions you plan to ask each vendor you're considering. Unfortunately, if you are a female you REALLY need to know what you are talking about because females are more likely to be given a higher quote than males. Sad, but true, I know this from experience. So all you females out there, get to know your stuff. That way no one can take advantage of you. In all the years I've owned and managed properties, men still try to over price me. Sorry, all my male readers, no disrespect to you, it is just a reality for women. An example of the questions to ask when you're building a plumber preferred vendor list include:

   a) Would you mind if I ask you some questions? I am in the process of building a vendor list with reliable and honest vendors, which I am sure you are, and I would like to add you to my list. (Be honest and upfront right from the beginning.)

   b) Do you repair leaky pipes?

   a) Do you repair broken/leaky faucets, underground pipes, clogged drains, etc. (This seems obvious if the vendor is a plumber, but you'd be surprised by what some vendors will or won't do. Ask the obvious questions *before* you hire them.)

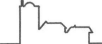
b)  What is the general cost for this type of work?

c)  Do you provide a warranty?

d)  How long does it usually take to do this type of repair?

e)  How long does it take from the time I make a service call to the time your technician arrives at my home?

2.  After you exhaust all your questions of that one vendor, pick three or more vendors and ask the same questions. You can find the vendors you're looking for on the Internet, *angieslist.com*, junk mail flyers, or a referral from a trusted friend, family member, or other property managers.

3.  Add the plumbers you felt satisfied with to your vendor list.

4.  If you call a plumber from your vendor list and he/she says they are booked until tomorrow, call the next one on your list until you find one that satisfies your needs.

5.  On the plumber's visit, you are not only inspecting the repair, you are also observing the plumber to see if he or she is good enough to be added to your preferred vendor list.

a)  When you make the appointment and when the vendor arrives take note of his or her personality – are they respectful? Did they get the job done efficiently? Did they try to over charge you or did they stay true to the price quoted?

b)  If you feel this plumber is exceptional, put the plumber on your preferred vendor list. If the plumber is not, he eithers stays on your vendor list or is removed completely, you decide.

Repeat these steps for every type of maintenance contractor or vendor you may need until you have a complete vendor and preferred vendor list.

**TIP**: No matter what type of repair I need I always get at least three estimates before I hire anyone. The one I choose is not necessarily the cheapest. The one I choose is the one that I feel is honest and reliable, but with a reasonable price. I'm always building my vendor list because some vendors stay and others go. You always need to have backups.

## Bed Bugs

Be aware of bedbugs. This has been a growing problem all over the country, but especially in California. It is expensive and difficult to get rid of bed bugs. ThermaPureHeat is an effective way to kill them because it can heat up to 113 degrees, which is the level of heat needed to kill bed bugs and their eggs. Companies like Coastal Risk Management (*www.coastalriskmanagement.com*) can help you get rid of these annoying pests. You can also call the California Department of Public Health and the California Department of Health Services. They can help you find successful, licensed, and experienced extermination companies.

I tell my tenants to be mindful of things they pick up at yard sales and thrift shops, especially if the item has fabric. Bed bugs can be transported by anyone on just about anything. Bed bugs have been such a problem in California, a new civil code has been established to address the issue. Civil Code Section 1954.603 states as of July 1, 2017, at the signing of a new tenant, landlords are required to provide specific information about bed bugs to a new tenant, and as of January 1, 2018, landlords are required to give the information to all other tenants, as well. (For bed bug information

and forms, visit *www.evict123.com/free-forms*, or request one by visiting my website at *www.simplyshiral.com.*)

## Summary

1. Add a *Tenant Maintenance & Repair Request* to your repairs policy and make sure your tenant provides you with one EVERY TIME a repair or scheduled maintenance is requested.

2. Make property inspections a part of your property management routine and remember to serve the tenant with a *Twenty-Four-Hour Notice of Intent to Enter* form before entering the tenant's unit to do the inspection.

3. Create a vendor list and preferred vendor list.

4. Always get at least three quotes from vendors before you hire someone for repairs or maintenance so you can compare prices.

5. Get up to speed on bed bugs.

Visit my website at *www.simplyshiral.com* and feel free to request any forms you need.

## Tenant Maintenance & Repair Request

Date: _____

Tenant's Name _____

Address _____

Problem/Repair Needed: _____

_____

_____

_____

_____

_____

Best time to make repairs: _____

By signing below, I authorized entry into my unit to perform the maintenance/repair request

Tenant's Signature: _____

Tenant's phone #: _____

**FOR MANAGEMENT USE ONLY:**

Scheduled Appointment: _____

Service Request Completed By: _____

Completion Date: _____

Comments: _____

_____

_____

_____

Signature Landlord/Manager _____

www.simplyshiral.com

## Vendor List

| Vendor | Contact Person | Number | Address | Website |
|--------|----------------|--------|---------|---------|
|  |  |  |  |  |
|  |  |  |  |  |
|  |  |  |  |  |
|  |  |  |  |  |
|  |  |  |  |  |
|  |  |  |  |  |
|  |  |  |  |  |
|  |  |  |  |  |
|  |  |  |  |  |
|  |  |  |  |  |
|  |  |  |  |  |
|  |  |  |  |  |

# Preferred Vendor List

| Vendor | Contact Person | Number | Address | Website |
|--------|----------------|--------|---------|---------|
|        |                |        |         |         |
|        |                |        |         |         |
|        |                |        |         |         |
|        |                |        |         |         |
|        |                |        |         |         |
|        |                |        |         |         |
|        |                |        |         |         |
|        |                |        |         |         |
|        |                |        |         |         |
|        |                |        |         |         |
|        |                |        |         |         |
|        |                |        |         |         |
|        |                |        |         |         |

www.simplyshiral.com

# Chapter Eleven: Evictions

Eviction is the one topic property owners dread, mainly because it takes time to get the tenant out of the unit, while not receiving any rent. Most evictions begin with a *Three-Day Notice to Vacate* in which the owner or manager serves the tenant. The steps after this notice should be done very carefully so the process can be completed accurately and as soon as possible. I would recommend hiring an attorney or eviction company to complete the process after you've served notice to your tenants.

This chapter covers the eviction process, required forms, and paves the way for a smoother eviction. Note that the information delivered in this chapter is for California properties only. If your rental is subject to Rent Control, call your local Rent Stabilization office or contact an eviction attorney for more information. If your rental is not in California, call an eviction attorney local to your rental, as your state may have a different process.

## Legal Advice

Most eviction law firms and companies provide the step-by-step eviction process and many have the information on their websites. Michael Brennan of Brennan Law Firm, *www.mbrennanlaw.com*, and Patti at Fast Eviction Service, *www.fastevictionservice.com,* are two in Los Angeles that I highly recommend.

Legal Shield is a company that provides free legal advice, plus they make phone calls and write letters on your behalf. They'll

also review an unlimited number of legal documents that are up to fifteen pages each, sometimes more if you are a member. Their membership fees are very low and are worth every penny. I've been a member of Legal Shield since 2002 and I use them personally and for my business.

## Evictions Reports Sealed in California

As of January 1, 2017, California passed a ridiculous law called AB 2819 Unlawful Detainer Masking Law that seals people's eviction histories. To put this in layman terms, a tenant's eviction report is sealed, and as a result, a prospective landlord never sees it. That means if we landlords do a credit check on a potential tenant, any evictions prospective tenant may have will not be listed on the report.

This is such an injustice to landlords.

## Here's How It Works

Typically, an eviction is not on a tenant's record within the first sixty days of eviction, because the eviction has not yet been recorded. If the landlord wins the eviction case within sixty days and does not sign a statement saying that the landlord will not seal the eviction records, then the records won't be sealed.

So you may think, note to self, I will not sign a document that states that I will seal the eviction report, right?

Wrong! You may have no choice but to sign the document because if you won't, then the tenant's attorney may opt to have a jury trial to make you sign.

So ultimately you have a choice between signing the form in the first place and ending the case, or not signing the form and going

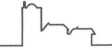
to trial, which will cost you thousands of dollars. Either way, the landlord is screwed.

If this freaks you out, know that I have owned rentals since 1997 and I have assisted others with evictions, but I've never had to do an eviction for any of my own rentals. Anything can happen, but you lessen your odds of evictions if you are diligent in learning more about this business (and your tenants before they move in), and then applying what you learn to your rental management business.

## Rent Control

By now I've drilled into you that everything is different if your rental property falls under the Rent Stabilization Ordinance a.k.a. Rent Control. I don't want to get into much detail with this subject because there is so much involved. But I do want to touch on the topic of single-family homes. Most people who own and live in a Rent Control area are aware that single-family homes do not fall under the Rent Stabilization Ordinance. However, a single-family home is affected by this ordinance if the owner rents out any of the bedrooms for over thirty days. Doing so automatically puts you in a position of having a multi-unit property. You would then fall under the Rent Stabilization Ordinance, and therefore fall under the jurisdiction of Rent Control.

So be mindful of the decisions you make and don't let the very popular Airbnb option entice you without first learning all the pros and cons. If you decided to rent out a bedroom, I would suggest that you don't rent it out for more than thirty days. For more details, contact your local Rent Stabilization office.

## Gather Before Starting

The longer it takes for you to prepare for your eviction, the longer it takes to get your tenant out. So before you call an attorney and start the eviction process, gather the following information to make the process run smoother and more efficiently.

1.  Name of legal owner of building. (Is it you personally or your business?)

2.  Your mailing and email address.

3.  Tenants' names (everyone living there, who pays the rent, and signed the lease).

4.  Address of the eviction (including the apt number).

5.  Current rent amount and the day it is due.

6.  Amount of rent currently owed.

7.  The rental agreement. (Is it written or oral?)

8.  Is the unit subject to rent control?

9.  Was the tenant served a notice? If yes, what type? (For example, *Notice to Pay Rent or Move, Three-day Notice to Cure Violation.*)

    Forms are available online, through your local landlord association, or you can get them by visiting my website at *www.simplyshiral.com* and request the one you need.

10. If the tenant was served a notice, what was the date it was served and how was the notice served? (By you? If by a third party, who was it?)

11. Amount of rent requested on the notice (if applicable).

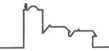 

## Eviction Process

Whatever the reason is that you decide to evict a tenant, you must start by serving your tenant a notice. For example, if the tenant does not pay their rent on the day it is due, you must send them a *Three-Day-Notice-To-Pay-Rent-Or-Move*. If the tenant does not pay their rent by the end of the time period of the notice, then it is time to start an eviction, also known as an *Unlawful Detainer*, with the Superior Court. You may be able to do this yourself, but I recommend you hire an eviction attorney like Michael Brennan Law Office or Fast Eviction Services (both in the Los Angeles area).

**TIP:** There are so many *dos* and *don'ts* to this process that if you make a mistake, it will delay the outcome. If you use an attorney, it will get done professionally and timely because these attorneys know the process inside and out. And the quicker the tenant is out the sooner you can rent out the unit.

Once the eviction is filed with the court, the tenant has about two weeks to respond and appear, depending on if the eviction is uncontested or contested. The examples of each that I give below are for the state of California only. Be sure to check with the county and state in which your property resides for the types of evictions available to you, as your state may have a different process.

## Uncontested Eviction

After you start the eviction, the tenants determine if your eviction is an uncontested or contested eviction. An uncontested eviction is when the tenant doesn't respond to the court after the two-week period from the *Unlawful Detainer* filing date. This shortens the eviction process because there is no need for a trial. The tenant is

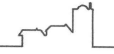

in the wrong by default due to nonresponse. Most often the cost of the eviction is lower when it's uncontested.

## Contested Eviction

On the other hand, a contested eviction is when the tenant responds and decides to fight the case. As a result, a trial date is set in which both sides will appear in front of a judge. On your side, either the property owner (you), your property manager, or a legal representative such an attorney will present your case. You do not need to have an attorney represent you, but I highly recommend that you do.

## Forms

Below are some of the common forms you may need to help you in the eviction process. These are forms you should have on-hand as a property owner or manager. You can get these forms for free if you belong to a landlord association or you can download them for free at *www.mbrennanlaw.com*, *www.fastevictionservice.com*, or visit my website at *www.simplyshiral.com* and request the one you need.

1. Three Day Notice to Pay Rent or Move
2. Three Day Notice to Move
3. Thirty/Sixty Day to Vacate
4. Declaration of Service of Notice(s) to Tenant(s)
5. Notice to Enter Dwelling Unit
6. Notice to Perform or Quit

## STORY TIME

My friend had a tenant, but did not use a rental agreement. After living there for six months the tenant

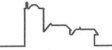
stopped paying rent. Even though my friend didn't have a rental agreement with the tenant, she still needed to start the eviction process. First, she served the tenant a *Three-Day-Notice-To-Pay-Rent-Or-Move*. The tenant did not pay the rent on the third day so she started the eviction with an eviction attorney. The eviction attorney filed the *Unlawful Detainer* with the court. My friend thought this would be a simple eviction and that the tenant would just move after being served by the court. Instead, the tenant *did* respond to the notice and after months and months of rescheduled court dates, loss of rents, and $25,000 in legal fees the tenant finally gave up and agreed to move out.

At last my friend was able to re-rent the unit and start receiving rental income again. Lesson learned.

## Summary

1. Retain a legal advice company that you can contact on an as-needed basis.

2. Learn about the eviction process and how sealed evictions work.

3. Gather the required information you need *before* starting the eviction process. Time is money!

4. Have the required eviction forms on hand so there is no delay in serving a tenant.

If you don't belong to a Landlord Association, you can download them for free at *www.mbrennanlaw.com, www.fastevictionservice.com,* or visit my website at *www.simplyshiral.com* and request the one you need.

# Chapter Twelve:
# Recordkeeping & Bookkeeping

Recordkeeping and bookkeeping are so important that they need their own chapter. This task, if not done at least monthly, can cause an array of problems, such as lost income, unexplained expenses, missing or misplaced documents, the list goes on. Accurate and consistent recordkeeping and bookkeeping are the backbone of a successful business. I've met many mom-and-pop owners who don't use any type of record or bookkeeping system. If you are like them, this chapter will be especially helpful. Bookkeeping doesn't have to be complicated. It just needs to be done on a consistent basis. This chapter gives you the basics on what a record and book-keeping system is and how to start one.

## Recordkeeping

Recordkeeping is simply keeping track of the history of one's activities, such as financial dealings, by entering data in ledgers, filing documents, updating journals, etc. This can be a very complex topic if you don't organize, store, or keep documents all together. As I mentioned in Chapter Nine, I use the binder system, and in doing so I have a binder for each property I own and I have a system to keep everything organized. I have a table of contents for each binder to help stay organized no matter which binder I happen to be using.

## Fijitsu Scanner

This may sound like an odd topic to add to this chapter, but *let me tell you*, other than my computer and my printer, my Fujitsu Scan Snap scanner (ScanSnap S5100) is one of my most treasured tools in my office. (I have model S5100, but they have many other models that you might want to consider.) When my friend and colleague, Leslie Crumley, and I discovered this device, we were on top of the world. Yes, considering we are both a little nuts when it comes to organization, not to mention OCD, I think my scanner is a device that is overlooked by most people who are trying to get organized. We use it every day to scan documents, receipts, and invoices just to name a few. We store our scanned documents in the computer so we have less paperwork to file, which eliminates the need to make photocopies, saves paper, and frees up yet another file cabinet in your office.

**TIP**: I have tried many different brands of scanners and found that the cost of a Fujitsu scanner is a little higher than others, but well worth it. I have had mine for years and their customer service staff (you actually talk to a person when you call) are top notch (*www.fujitsu.com*).

## Bookkeeping

The definition of bookkeeping is *the work or skill of keeping account books or systematic records of money transactions*. Whether you own one rental, many rentals, manage your property yourself, or hire a property manager, you must keep accurate records of your income and expenses. There are many types of software programs like Quicken and QuickBooks that property management companies

use to do their bookkeeping. If you manage your properties yourself, and don't want to use a computer software program, a simple spreadsheet will do the trick.

I have found that many mom-and-pop owners collect rents and deposit that income into their personal accounts. I don't recommend this at all. Mixing business with personal money makes it difficult to separate your personal income and expenses with your business income and expenses. Thus, making tax preparation much more challenging and opening the door to overlooking deductible receipts. The simple worksheet I have developed makes it easy for anyone to keep track of income and expenses on a monthly basis. I have included a sample income and expense spreadsheet at the end of this chapter. If you need further help, visit my website at *www.simplyshiral.com* to check out my workshops, or contact me directly at *shiral@simplyshiral.com* to ask your questions.

## STORY TIME

When we first started purchasing rental properties, being the OCD organized person that I am, I had to figure out how I was going to keep track of the rents and the bills. So with a pencil, I drew a bunch of lines on a blank piece of paper and made columns separating the rents from the bills. This is what I did for the first five years. Little did I know, all that time I had been drawing a spreadsheet. Why didn't I know? I wasn't a business major, nor did I know anything about business. I was a counselor in the field of substance abuse treatment.

But oh my gosh, when I learned how to use Microsoft Excel it opened up so many doors for me. After that I created spreadsheets for everything I could think of, and before I knew it, I developed personal budgets, projected budgets, forms, you name it, I created it.

Computers...sometimes they make you so mad you want to throw them out the window and other times you can't believe all the things you can do with them. My computer is one of my best friends and it has helped me organize, stay organized, and overall made my life so much simpler.

## Summary

1. Understand the difference between recordkeeping and bookkeeping so that you keep accurate business records.

If you need help creating a budget, tracking income/expenses, or using a budget, contact me through my website at *www.simplyshiral.com*.

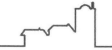

# Income & Expense Tracking

| Income | Pay Date | Deposit to | Jan | Feb | Mar | Apr | May | Jun | Jul | Aug | Sep | Oct | Nov | Dec | Yearly Totals |
|---|---|---|---|---|---|---|---|---|---|---|---|---|---|---|---|
| | | | | | | | | | | | | | | | |
| | | | | | | | | | | | | | | | |
| | | | | | | | | | | | | | | | |
| | | | | | | | | | | | | | | | |
| | | | | | | | | | | | | | | | |
| **Total Income** | | | | | | | | | | | | | | | |

| Expenses | Due Date | Paid from | Jan | Feb | Mar | Apr | May | Jun | Jul | Aug | Sep | Oct | Nov | Dec | Yearly Totals |
|---|---|---|---|---|---|---|---|---|---|---|---|---|---|---|---|
| | | | | | | | | | | | | | | | |
| | | | | | | | | | | | | | | | |
| | | | | | | | | | | | | | | | |
| | | | | | | | | | | | | | | | |
| | | | | | | | | | | | | | | | |
| | | | | | | | | | | | | | | | |
| | | | | | | | | | | | | | | | |
| | | | | | | | | | | | | | | | |
| | | | | | | | | | | | | | | | |
| | | | | | | | | | | | | | | | |
| | | | | | | | | | | | | | | | |
| Misc. Expenses Total | | | | | | | | | | | | | | | |
| **Total Expenses** | | | | | | | | | | | | | | | |

| | | | | | | | | | | | | | | | |
|---|---|---|---|---|---|---|---|---|---|---|---|---|---|---|---|
| **Total Income** | | | | | | | | | | | | | | | |
| **Total Expenses** | | | | | | | | | | | | | | | |
| **Grand Total** | | | | | | | | | | | | | | | |

www.simplyshiral.com

89

# Chapter Thirteen: Tips That Improve Your Rental Business

There are so many tips in the field of investment real estate and property management that I felt there needed to be a chapter that solely covers as many as I could think of, listed in no particular order. These tips will save you so much time, money, stress, and they are very easy to implement into your business. I learned these tips the hard way and I am passing them on to you so you can avoid some of the challenges I went through in my early years.

## Lower Insurance Premiums

Paying homeowner's insurance is an expense that you cannot eliminate if you borrowed money from a bank to purchase your property. (Even if you didn't you should still insure your home.) But you can control the cost of your insurance premium. If you raise your deductible, your annual homeowner's insurance premium goes down. For example, if your deductible is $500 have your insurance agent raise it to $1,000 and you'll be surprised by how much you save. Before doing this, however, make sure you have the amount of your deductible in your cash reserves just in case you need to make a claim.

## Credit Cards

Do you have balances on multiple credit cards you want to pay off? Follow the steps below in my Snowball Effect to systematically pay down your credit cards until they're balance free:

1. Write down a list off all your credit cards and order them starting with the card that has the lowest balance at the top down to the card with the highest balance at the bottom.

2. Every month pay the minimum payment for each card, except pay extra on the top card (which has the lowest balance).

3. When the top card is paid off, continue to pay the minimum payment on all the cards except for the top card on the list, which was previously the second card. Make the minimum payment on that new top card, but add the amount you were paying on the original first card (the one you paid off). You will pay this second card off much sooner because it includes not only its minimum payment but also the payment of the original top card.

4. When the second card is paid off do the same thing to the third card, including not only its minimum payment but also the payment for the first and second cards (now both paid off).

5. Continue steps 1 through 4 every month until all your credit cards have a zero balance.

I call this the Snowball Effect. You will see how quickly you pay off your cards if you use this strategy. Of course, this only works if

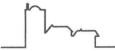 

you STOP using your credit cards while paying them down. The trick is, don't charge them back up again to get yourself in the same predicament.

## Welcome Gift

It's always a nice gesture to purchase your new tenant a *welcome* or *happy move in* gift. You may ask yourself, *why should I give my tenant a gift? Aren't they lucky to be living in my property in the first place?*

Well, think about this: A simple and kind gesture goes a long way. There may come a time when you need your tenant to cut you some slack. If you leave your new tenant a *welcome* gift, like a plant, a gift card, or a bottle of Martinelli's Sparkling Cider, that tenant will remember you as a thoughtful and generous person. Think about it…that could be helpful down the road.

## Sorry for the Inconvenience Gift

There will most likely be a time when you will have to do something that will be an inconvenience to your tenants. For example, my tenant called me one day and said that overnight her water heater leaked all over her kitchen floor and into the carpet in the living room. This could have been a disaster, but my tenant was very patient. To fix the leak, our plumber went over immediately to put in a new water heater. So that was taken care of.

But we still had the soaked carpet to deal with. Our carpet cleaner came over to extract the water and put two fans in the living room to help the carpet dry and avoid mold. The tenant had to leave the fans on for about five days. This tenant didn't complain even once. Because we were so grateful for her patience, we gave her a Ralphs Supermarket gift card as a thank you for being so nice about the inconvenience this may have been on her and her family.

## Happy Holidays

We are very grateful to our tenants because as I said before, they are the ones who pay our mortgage. As a holiday gift, we reduce our tenants' rent by way of a holiday card that we send out on December first that states what their reduced rent will be for one month in the month of January. We tell our tenants that it's a holiday gift for the New Year so that we are respectful of all ethnic holidays, religions, and non-religion families.

## Rent Control

As I have been saying throughout this book repeatedly, if you purchase properties in a Rent Control area (a.k.a. Rent Stabilization), read about it, keep up with laws, and attend any meetings about it. Rent Control is a complex and frustrating ordinance that can end up costing you a lot of money if you don't stay on top of the associated laws. It pays to make your education of your local rental laws an ongoing process.

## In Fact, Keep Up with All the Laws

I can't stress enough staying on top of all rental property, property management, and tax laws, regardless of Rent Control. I meet so many owners who don't make educating themselves a priority. If you break a law and are served with a lawsuit it can become very expensive, because a judge will almost never let you slide just

because you were unaware of the law. It's your responsibility to keep yourself informed.

## Don't Rent to Family and Friends

My parents had two rentals while I was growing up and they taught me one valuable lesson that has stuck with me: Never, ever rent to family and friends. They had to learn this the hard way. Relationships with family and friends can be tested when someone asks for favors.

For example, if a family member or friend who is a renter cannot pay the rent one month, they may think you will let them slide. And when you don't, then you have a problem between the two of you. They don't realize that you need their rent to pay your mortgage. Issues like this (trust me there are even more) puts a strain on the relationship.

In the end, it's not worth risking it. Rent only to well-qualified strangers so that you can keep your friends and family relationships healthy.

## Open a Separate Bank Account

Having a separate bank account for your personal finances and your rental properties makes bookkeeping and tax preparation much simpler. I always tell my students, "Don't comingle your business funds with your personal accounts." Doing so makes it much more difficult to prepare for income tax and (most importantly) getting all those deductions in.

Also, it's a good idea to put all your rental property security deposits in a separate account. At some point your tenant will move out and you will have to come up with a chunk of money in order

to give back their security deposit. You don't want to be caught without those funds.

## Home Owners Association A.K.A. HOA

Don't confuse an HOA with landlord associations. Know that if you buy property that has an HOA, the HOA fee will (in most cases) increase as the years go on.

An HOA is usually part of a planned community, like a condo complex or housing development. The HOA pays for common amenities like landscaping, a recreational center (such as a pool), and outside building repairs (like when a new roof is needed). If you buy property with an HOA, you cannot extract yourself from the HOA so include any HOA fees as part of your costs when you do your budget and when you determine what you want to charge for rent.

If one of your goals with your rentals is to use them as income, keep in mind that you don't know what the exact HOA fee will be in the long-term future (for example, five years from now). But always account for it because it will always be there.

## STORY TIME

The fourth rental we purchased was a condo in Newberg, Oregon. Newberg is a beautiful city with the kind of weather we love; green, overcast, and rainy. We bought this with the idea that we would use it as a vaca-tion home/rental when we retire.

As the years went on, the HOA fees on our little Newberg getaway started to rise. Within a two-year period, they went from sixty-seven dollars a month to

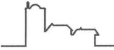

almost two hundred dollars a month. Since the rent was only seven hundred dollars, I realized that in ten years the HOA fees would be almost as much as the rent.

Before making the decision to sell it, I took a position on the HOA Board of Directors as the secretary. I wanted to learn more about the HOA, all the condos in general, and the financials of the building. One thing I found out blew me away. If a unit went into foreclosure or short sale, the rest of the owners in the condo complex had to incur the failing condo's HOA fees. This had the high risk to be obscenely expensive, given it was 2008 when foreclosures and short sales were happening everyday all across the United States.

I loved that condo and was looking forward to using it later in life, but after learning everything I needed to know by being on the HOA board, we decided that selling our condo was the best decision. If we had kept it, our expenses would have eventually exceeded the income.

## Legal Advice

I believe it is important to get as much legal advice as you can. You can always get your own attorney, but before you do that, just know that there are less expensive resources available to you.

As I mentioned before, law groups like Legal Shield provide legal services for a small monthly fee. Members have access to legal counsel and advice from qualified lawyers, paralegals, and much more. Visit their website at *www.legalshield.com* for more information, or

google "legal help" and check out the options that come up in the search.

Landlord magazines provide legal advice in every issue. They are easy reading with short stories and are very relatable. The Legal Q&A pages in *Apartment Owners Association Magazine* and the Legal Corner column in *Apartment Management Magazine* are a must-read. I look forward to reading them every month.

Landlord associations like Apartment Owners Association (*www.aoausa.com*) give advice and refer you to their top attorneys. These attorneys answer your questions at no cost.

## Hire an Accountant

I suggest you hire a qualified accountant who knows real estate tax law, and not that cheap tax guy up the street, around the corner, in that hole in the wall office space who guarantees refunds. You know the one I'm talking about; that guy who messes with the numbers to get you a refund (whether you deserve one or not) so you will come back to him next year. Yes, that guy! Where is he when you're audited?

Just hire a real accountant, a CPA, or a tax attorney so you will feel safe if you're ever audited. It will save money, time, and stress in the long run.

## Don't Give Tenants Your Address

If you took my advice when I said don't rent to friends and family, then it stands to reason that your tenants are strangers, and as such you really don't want them to know where you physically live. Get a US Post Office box, UPS box, or any other mail service that gives you a mailing address so you don't have to use your primary

residence when corresponding with your tenants by mail. Why? You don't want your tenants coming over at all hours of the day or night just to tell you they are going to be late with their rent or to discuss any other issues they may have. They can call or text you.

## Separate Your Wants and Needs

I know you really *want* that fancy Kohler pewter-plated faucet, but it costs twice as much as a regular, generic brand faucet that works just as well, so do you really *need* the extravagant Kohler one? Will the tenant even appreciate it?

Sometimes it is best to get basics instead of the expensive fancy stuff for rentals, because tenants are not always going to value and appreciate the higher end versions. And even if they do, your tenants may not align with your taste.

You don't have to buy cheap fixtures or materials, just know you don't have to get the most expensive ones, either. Really think about what you *need* versus what you *want* before you buy.

## Build a Cash Reserve and Don't Spend It

This seems like common sense, but I have met so many owners who have lost their properties or have gotten into credit card debt because they splurged their cash reserves on unnecessary things. You want to build a cash reserve to have the funds available when you have a large ticket item that needs to be taken care of.

For example, if it is raining and your tenant calls to tell you the roof is leaking, you will have to rely on your reserves to pay for it right then and there – not six months from now after you've saved up for it. Otherwise you will have to put emergency repairs on a

credit card and that creates a whole new problem, namely credit card debt and unnecessary interest.

## Buy in Bulk

If you're at your local Home Depot or Costco to purchase a smoke detector for one of your units, and you find it's on sale, and you know your other units will need smoke detectors replaced in the near future, buy them all now to take advantage of the sale. Buying in bulk also saves you from another trip to Home Depot, Costco, or any other home center you use.

On top of that, some home center stores (both big box and online) give a discount when purchasing the same item in multiples. It pays to check before you buy.

## Quarterly or Annual Inspections

Depending on where your property exists, you may be susceptible to regular home inspections by your local city or county government. Regardless, you want to inspect your properties at least once a year to stay on top of normal wear-and-tear repairs.

When inspection times come up, make sure you give your tenants at least a *Twenty-Four-Hour Notice to Enter* form (at least twent-four hours in advance) before inspecting their unit. Check the plumbing for leaks and water pressure, test smoke/carbon monoxide detectors, look for bugs, and examine the overall look of the unit. Create a checklist that includes the items you want to review before doing the inspection.

Another reason for doing ongoing inspections is if a tenant knows you are taking a look at things on a regular basis, they

will most likely take better care of their unit and make sure it is always tidy.

## Dealing with Tenant Issues

Always, I mean *always*, treat your tenants with respect regardless of how mad they make you (or how mad they are at you). Deal with issues as a professional business person. If you let your emotions get involved, you may say something rude, discriminatory, or out of line. This type of tension is not worth it for you or your tenant. Keep a lid on your anger and be as respectful as possible to the people who rent your property. Without your renters, you wouldn't have any rental income!

## Back Up Your Data on Your Computer

If you store any of your documents, forms, or tenant files on your computer, make sure you back them up on something like an external hard drive, Dropbox, the Cloud, or any other safe storage outside of your computer. I say this because, when I was on Chapter Seven of writing this book, my computer was hit with a virus that corrupted all my files. I was thankful and grateful that I had most of my files on an external hard drive and flash drives. Even though I only lost about three months of work, it was still devastating. If I didn't have this book on a flash drive and found it as one of my corrupted files, this book would not be here today. So make sure you back up your files!

## Your Time Is Valuable

My friend, colleague, and personal finance strategist, Leslie Crumley (*www.structuredsuccess.com*) would always say to me, "Your time is valuable." I never really understood what she meant until a few years ago.

Every time someone asked me questions related to real estate investing, property management, and money management, I would spend hours teaching them how I do things and what worked for me. Though I spent over $30,000 for my real estate education, I never charged anyone a dime to share my knowledge. I always thought if they ask me after work hours and I'm free anyway, then why not.

Years later, I started teaching one-on-ones and workshops for free, and again, Leslie said to me, "Your time is valuable."

Finally, years later I noticed that all the people I gave a free education to were not taking action. This, of course, frustrated me because when they got into a bind, they would come back to me with questions I'd already answered in my free workshops. After a while I started feeling that since they were not using any of my education, they were wasting my time.

And that's when I finally understood what Leslie had been telling me for years. Right then and there I decided to charge a small fee for my one-on-ones and workshops. It was then when I finally saw people take action.

When I gave my knowledge away for free, it wasn't looked at as valuable – not until I started charging for it. It's crazy because the education I offer is the same whether I charge for it or not.

The lesson here is this: *Your time is valuable.* So make sure you use it wisely.

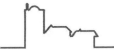 

## Don't be Fooled by the Numbers

There are always hidden costs that you need to know about. Years ago, when I first started teaching, I would figure out my true costs by using this formula:

*Workshop fee minus cost of supplies and space rental equals profit.*

For example, workshop fee is $100 minus supplies and rent of $40, equals $60 in profit. I used this formula for years until Leslie Crumley, personal finance strategist, helped me understand that I need to add self-employment tax and transportation expenses to my cost. She said that I don't' see the effects of those expenses until I file my taxes.

For those of you out there who use basic formulas (like I did), yet want to know your true costs, talk to a financial strategist like Leslie (*www.structuredsuccess.com*). Professionals like her are well worth the time, effort, and money.

## Mortgage Paydown

You can save thousands of dollars in mortgage interest and decrease the amount of years left on your mortgage simply by modifying your house payment every month. How you do that depends on a lot of factors such as the balance left on your mortgage, your interest rate, your regular mortgage payment, and your income. Rather than give you a one-size-fits-all strategy, book a free thirty-minute phone consultation with me by going to my website at *www.simplyshiral.com* and I'll show you how you can pay off your mortgage quicker AND save thousands of dollars. Believe me, it's worth it!

## Trust Yourself

As my last tip, I want you to truly trust yourself. Many outside sources claim to know this business inside and out, they think they have all the answers, and yet they don't even own rentals properties. What kind of mentor is that? Please don't take advice from them. Do your own research and consider all the things you learn in this book. Talk to other people who have been on the front line with investment properties, and then simply trust yourself. Listen to your intuition. No one will take better care of your properties than you.

## Summary

1. Consider using tips that save you money like raising your insurance deductible and paying off your credit cards.

2. Make time to learn about current real estate, rental property, and tax laws.

3. Treat your rental properties as the business that it is. Use my tips (and others you find) to separate your business from your personal life.

4. Consider giving your tenant a *welcome* gift, gift cards for unexpected repairs, and holiday discounts.

Once you do all of your homework, trust yourself and your instinct so you can enjoy the process.

# Chapter Fourteen: Income

Income is the number one reason we invest in rental properties. Whether the property is used as a means for monthly income, an inheritance for children, retirement, or just simply because it is a hobby, we need income in order to make this real estate wheel turn. Therefore, you need to know ways to gain and save income through your rental properties. That's primarily through collecting rent, of course, but then you have to know what to do with that rent and how to hold on to it.

## Rent

Do you review your rents annually? Researching rents in the area your rentals are located gives you an idea of what rents should be. How do you research rents, you may ask? Many will tell you to look on the Internet, ask a realtor, or check with a local landlord association. Personally, I don't rely on the Internet because most of these websites only give averages or a range. I want numbers that are much more precise.

What many mom-and-pop rental businesses don't realize is that rental averages may not be true to the neighborhood their rental is in because rents can vary from city to city and neighborhood to neighborhood.

So how do I find out this information?

Remember, I'm into Old School techniques. I drive up and down the area in which my rentals reside and I take down phone numbers of buildings similar to ours that are for rent. I then call up the owners, as a prospective tenant, to find out what they are renting their units for. This approach gives a more current and accurate amount of what the rents are in my neighborhood.

## Rents Due on the First

All my rents are due on the first day of the month as a way to simplify my bookkeeping and to ensure I have the funds to pay my mortgages, which are also due on the first. But if a tenant does not move in on the first, then you must prorate the tenant's rent. There are two positives to prorating rents, as opposed to making rent due on the same day every month as the day the tenant moved in:

1. Landlord receives all rents, from all properties, on the same day, which is the first day of the month.

2. Lower move-in amount for the renter which makes your vacancy much more appealing.

Below is an example of how to prorate rents to the first day of the month. Let's say the tenant moving in does so under these parameters.

- The tenant's move in day is October 8.
- Monthly rent is $1,000.
- Security deposit is $1,000.

Since the month of October has thirty-one days, you use this formula to find out how much it costs to live in your rental unit for a day:

Divide the total amount of rent by the number of days in the month, in this case it looks like this: $1,000 ÷ 31 days = $32.26 per day to live in your unit.

- Since the tenant will be moving in on October 8, the tenant will not be charged for the first seven days of the month. The tenant will be charged only for twenty-four days which is from the October 8 to October 31 as follows: $32.26 x 24 days = $774.24 to move in.

Therefore, your tenant's total move-in fees are as follows:

- $774.24 – Tenant's rent for the month of October
- $1,000.00 – Security Deposit
- $1,774.24 – Total move in amount for tenant

## Counterfeit Money

Be aware that unfortunately there is counterfeit money out there. If you accept your rent in cash, your odds of receiving counterfeit money rises. If you bring a counterfeit bill to the bank, the bank will confiscate the bill and not replace it with a real one, whether you knew it was counterfeit or not (which of course, you did not know when you accepted it, otherwise you wouldn't have accepted it).

For this reason, I do not accept cash from renters. I only accept a check, money order, or cashier's check. Let me repeat, *if a tenant gives you a counterfeit bill and you don't know it, and you go to the bank to try to deposit it, the bank will take it and will not replace it.*

## Laundry Room

If you have a multi-unit property and don't have a laundry room, you are losing out on some cash. Companies like CSC Service Works not only provide the laundry equipment, they also keep the machines maintained, collect all the money, and send you (the owner) your share. With a laundry service like this, the landlord does not have to do any upkeep or maintenance of the laundry machines. If something goes wrong with the washer or dryer a tenant or the landlord makes a call to the company and someone comes out to fix the equipment at no cost to the owner.

## STORY TIME

I hear from many Landlords that it is tough for them to find good tenants that pay their rent on time because if rents don't come in, there is no income for them to pay their bills. We have been pretty lucky finding good tenants that pay on time...wait a minute, let me knock on wood before I continue this story. OK, I'm done.

Getting back to my story, on the day of signing a new tenant, I, being the more serious half in my marriage, get all the signing of the move-in paperwork done with the tenant. My husband, on the other hand, is the muscle of the two of us. He does "the bro thing." For example, if one of the tenants is a young guy, my husband will take him aside and say, "Hey bro, we keep our rents low, we respect our tenants' space, and in return we expect that you abide by the rental agreement, be respectful of the neighbors and pay your rent

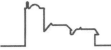 

on time." He says it in a polite, but *Don't @#$% with me* kind of attitude and it works. Our tenants pay their rent on time and are very respectful. I think because we are honest with them, and they know we are regular people paying bills just like them, they comply.

## Save Your Income

In the property management game, we always have repairs. How can we reduce our repair cost so we can save income? Personally, I can think of one way you can save income. *When it comes to repairs, do them yourself.*

Many investors will disagree with me on this, but we come from having no money. For us to be able to buy more properties, we had to save as much income as we could. Once we were able to save up a cash reserve account, and acquire more properties, then we were able to hire out and not do repairs ourselves.

My dad taught me at a young age how to build, repair, and have a creative mind. If he didn't know how to fix something, he would figure it out and then he taught me how to do the same. Once we started owning properties, the question we received most from other property owners was, "Who's your handyman?"

"You're lookin' at her!" I would reply.

My husband would comically say, "I don't know how to fix things like my wife does, but I know how to use a broom and dust pan."

When I was in my thirties my dad passed away, and sadly I no longer had him to go to when I needed to learn how to fix something.

But then I discovered Lowe's and Home Depot. They offer free workshops on many topics. What's great about going to a training class at a home store is that they sell everything you need to do the task. Today you can learn how to do just about anything on the Internet or on YouTube. Habitat for Humanity is also a great resource. Volunteers not only contribute to building homes for families, they also learn (and share) valuable skills while helping a great cause.

## Refinance Your Loan

You can save income by refinancing your mortgage after a few years of owning your property. Check the interest rate on your mortgage every few years and compare your interest rate to the current home mortgage rates lending institutions offer. If your rate is higher, call your accountant or bank and ask if it would make sense for you to refinance your mortgage. The danger in doing this, however, is that most people refinance for another thirty years to make the monthly payment lower. Depending on your goals, you might want to think about this. How old will you be thirty years from now when you finally pay off your mortgage?

Our rentals are our retirement, so the longer it takes to pay off our mortgage loans, the longer it will be before we can retire. Therefore, if we refinanced our loans, we make sure the amount of years left on our new loan is the same as our current loan. Using this strategy, we are guaranteed our new mortgage loan will be paid off the same time as our current loan.

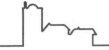

## Raise Your Insurance Deductible

This was one of my tips in the previous chapter, but it's such a good way to hold on to income it's worth repeating. Do you know anyone who has made an insurance claim on their home? I don't. So I asked my insurance agent, "If I raise the deductible on our property insurance, will our monthly premiums (which is another word for payments) be reduced?"

He replied, "Yes."

That was easy. I immediately raised the deductibles on the insurance policies on all our properties so we could keep more of our income. I would only suggest doing this, however, if you have the required deductible amount saved in your reserves, just in case you really did have to make a claim on your property due to damage.

## Summary

1. Annually research the rents in the areas in which your rentals reside.

2. Prorate the first month's rent payment so that all of your rents are due on the first day of the month.

3. Be aware that counterfeit money is out there. Don't accept cash as a payment for rent.

4. Explore professional laundry services that provide machines and maintenance for your rental properties.

5. Brainstorm on additional (unconventional) ways to raise and keep the income you receive.

# Chapter Fifteen: Expenses

In the previous chapter we learned about the wonderful word *income*. I wish we could keep all of it, but we can't because we have this thing called *expenses*. Expenses are all the bills, repairs, maintenance, and everything else you need to keep your business going. But like income, expenses also have an upside called *deductions*.

A deduction is an expense that you get to subtract from your taxable income, thus allowing you to pay less taxes. Almost all expenses related to the rental property business are tax deductible. This chapter covers some of the more common expense items on the IRS Schedule E form that help reduce your taxes. Most of the information below is on the IRS website so if you would like to learn more, visit *www.irs.gov*.

As I mentioned in previous chapters, it is important for you to understand that I am not an accountant or tax attorney, so everything I do and everything I write about is from real-life experiences (my stories).

With that in mind, let's get to finding some deductions to reduce your tax!

## Schedule E Form

How do you let the IRS know about your deductions? You list them on the IRS Schedule E form. This form allows you to report income or loss from rental real estate, royalties, partnerships,

S corporations, and just about any other type of business venture. Remember, you must keep records to support all items you report on your Schedule E in case the IRS has questions about them after you file your taxes. If the IRS asks you to produce something to substantiate one of your deductions and you don't have it, you may have to pay a penalty.

Below are the common items listed under Expenses on the Schedule E form. I will give a brief description of each deductible item. According to the Internal Revenue Service, you can deduct all ordinary and necessary expenses, including insurance, taxes, management fees, and depreciation. You can also deduct the items listed below, but sometimes it gets tricky if you don't have the proper documentation, so keep all your receipts!

## Advertising

You generally can deduct reasonable advertising expenses that are directly related to your rental property business such as advertising your vacant rental in the newspaper, online, or any other means to get the word out in the process of searching for a new tenant.

## Auto and Travel

You can deduct ordinary and necessary auto and travel expenses that relate to your rental properties, including public transportation (such as airline, train, or bus tickets), lodging fees, parking, tolls, and 50% of meal expenses incurred while traveling away from home. In most cases, you can either deduct your actual expenses or take the mileage rate if you use your car for business. Talk to your accountant for more information.

## Cleaning and Maintenance

You can deduct any fees related to cleaning a vacant unit, maintenance of appliances in your rental unit, annual property maintenance (like blowing out sprinklers or painting the building), or anything else that contributes to the betterment of your property. If it's a repair or necessary maintenance of your rental property, chances are you can deduct it on your Schedule E.

## Commissions

Commissions, bonuses, fees, and other amounts you pay to realtors, property managers, loan officers, and any professionals that help you lease your property are business costs. You must amortize these costs over the term of the lease, which is why it's very important that you keep track of the documents you get at the close of escrow. All of the fees you paid to buy your property are itemized on those closing documents. And those fees are deductible.

## Insurance

You can deduct homeowner's insurance, auto insurance, and any other insurances directly related to your rental property business. Some insurances are obvious deductions, some are not, so talk to your accountant for more information on which insurances you can deduct.

## Legal and Other Professional Fees

Legal and other professional fees such as tax advice, tax return preparation, professional business groups you pay to join, or any expense (other than federal taxes and penalties) you pay to resolve

a tax underpayment are all tax deductible. So make sure you get an invoice or receipt when you pay for these services, even if it's an ongoing service (like if you have an attorney on retainer).

## Management Fees

You can deduct all management expenses that are related to your rental property business, such as a property manager, the laundry rental fees (if you provide a washer and dryer for your tenants), a gardener, and homeowner's association fees.

## Mortgage Interest Paid to Bank

You can deduct the mortgage interest you pay on your rental property, as well as financing fees when you purchase your property or if you refinance later. However, when you refinance a rental property for more than the previous outstanding balance (to pull out some equity for example), then the interest on the portion of the new loan that exceeds the original loan cannot be deducted as a rental expense, UNLESS the extra amount you borrowed is used somehow on your rental property. Check with your accountant on this one.

## Other Interest

You can deduct any other interest that is related to your rental property.

## Repairs

You can deduct the amounts paid for repairs and maintenance. However, deductions for improvements are a little tricky. Repairs

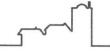

and maintenance costs keep the property in an ordinarily efficient operating condition. Examples are fixing a broken window or painting a bedroom. In contrast, improvements are amounts paid to better or restore your property or change it to a new or different use, like adding substantial insulation or replacing an entire HVAC system. Amounts paid to improve your property generally must be capitalized and depreciated (meaning they cannot be deducted in full in the year they are incurred). Check with your accountant before you take on any big improvements of your property to find out how you can get the best tax benefits.

## Supplies

In general, the cost of materials and supplies used for your rental property business may be deducted as a business expense in the tax year they are used. In addition, the cost of incidental materials and supplies that are kept on hand may be deducted in the tax year of purchase with certain guidelines. Remember to keep complete records and receipts for deductions for all supply expenses. Since many types of supplies can be used for personal use, refrain from deducting personal supplies as you can be given a penalty if caught by the IRS.

## Taxes

Taxes related to your rental property are also deductible. According to the IRS, deductible real estate taxes generally include any state, local, or foreign taxes on real property levied for the general public welfare. If a portion of your monthly mortgage payment goes into an escrow account, and periodically the lender pays your real estate

taxes out of the account to the local government, don't deduct the amount paid into the escrow account. Only deduct the amount actually paid out of the escrow account during the year to the taxing authority.

## Utilities

If your business is at home you can deduct a portion of your utility bills, but check with your accountant on how to figure out how much. If you pay for the utilities in your rental (in other words, your tenant does not pay the gas and electric bill – you do), then you can deduct those utilities, as well.

When it comes to your telephone, you can deduct the cost of phone calls related to your rental activities (for example, calls to the renter). However, the base rate (including taxes and other charges) for your local telephone service for the first telephone line into your residence is a personal expense and is not deductible.

## Depreciation Expense or Depletion

Depreciation is a capital expense. It is the mechanism use for recovering your cost in an income producing property and must be taken over the expected life of the property. Depreciation is tricky business, so it's best to talk to an accountant if you know you need to appreciate an expense over multiple years.

## Other

You can deduct many other ordinary and necessary expenses not listed here or even on the Schedule E for instructions. This is where it's handy to have a good accountant who knows tax law when it

comes to rental properties. A good accountant is well worth the money you pay him or her and can save you a lot of money in the long run.

## STORY TIME

Keeping our expenses at a minimal comes naturally to me, but the field of taxes does not. When we first started buying rentals, I had no idea taxes were involved. I wasn't raised in an environment that talked about money issues such as taxes. I'm embarrassed to say, I knew nothing about this topic. When I did our calculation before purchasing properties I created my own formula. It went like this: I take the rents and subtract expenses like mortgage, property tax, property insurance, utilities, maintenance, gardener, and a little for random expenses. Whatever was left was profit. If there was zero profit after I used my formula, I would skip it and move on to the next property until the numbers showed a profit.

When I learned more about real estate, and that expenses were deductions on a Schedule E form, and that the expenses lowered my income on a 1040, which then I paid less tax, of course I became interested and made it a point to learn a lot about taxes.

Now, years later, I have a better understanding of deductions and the tax benefits.

## Summary

1.  Understand that I am not a realtor, an attorney, or an accountant, so everything I do and everything I write about is from real-life experiences (my stories).

2.  Review all Schedule E items listed under expenses on the IRS website (*www.irs.gov*).

3.  Keep all records, documents, and receipts to support all the items you list on your Schedule E, just in case the IRS requests to see them.

# Chapter Sixteen: Simplicity

*Life is really simple, but we insist on making it complicated.*
Confucius

One of my favorite words, and one I try to live my life by, is SIMPLICITY. What a perfect chapter title on which to end my book. Technology, I thought, was supposed to make our lives simpler, but what I have witnessed is that we simply fill up the time technology saves making ourselves busier than ever. With computers, iPads, tablets, cell phones, texting, social media (the list goes on), we don't have time to enjoy day-to-day life experiences. In other words, there is no time to stop and smell the roses, or with my Hawaiian heritage, there is no time to smell the plumerias.

This chapter teaches you ways to simplify some tasks that are required of a rental property owner so that you can *take time to smell the plumerias.*

## Calendar

The use of a calendar will help you in so many ways to simplify your life. Choose the kind of calendar (for example, iCal, Google, a day planner, etc.) that works for you. I use a large desk calendar on my desk and a Google calendar on my computer. On day thirty of every month, I have a calendar item titled "Input next month's calendar items" because I manually update my calendar as a reminder. Most people today use electronic calendars or apps on

their smart phones. As I said before, I'm still somewhat Old School in many ways, which means I still use an old (i.e. not smart) phone that does not have access to Internet and email. Why? Because I don't feel I need one, so why should I get one? Maybe I will write another book someday called *How Going Old School Saves Money*.

Enter into your calendar your monthly and annual tasks like inspections and routine maintenance, for example checking the smoke/carbon monoxide detectors. Fill it in with upcoming tasks and daily activities so they will not be overlooked. Whether you choose to use a desk calendar, pocket calendar, or calendar app, you will find that it will simplify your life. I just find it comforting to go into my office every morning and look on my desk calendar to see what I will be doing for that day. Whatever works for you is fine, just make sure you get in the habit of using one because it will truly simplify your life.

## Home Warranty

If you really want to be able to sleep at night when it comes to your rental properties, buy a home warranty for each property. A home warranty company like American Home Shield or America's First Choice provides a service contract that covers the repairs or replacement of important home components and appliances that break down over time (like a washer, dryer, refrigerator, dishwasher, stove, furnace, just to name a few). Having a home warranty on your rental property can possibly save you time and money. They charge an annual fee and also a low service fee every time a technician has to come out to fix something. They will also replace an item if it can't be fixed. **Tip:** To save money on service fees for multi-unit properties, check with all your tenants before you do repairs for one tenant to see if anyone else needs similar repairs. For example,

if a tenant informs you that they have a plumbing issue, before calling your home warranty service, call all your other tenants to see if they also have plumbing issues. Home warranty companies charge one fee for all issues placed on one service request. This will save you lots of money. If you don't check with all your tenants first, and another tenant calls later with a plumbing issue, you will need to pay another service fee for that new work order.

For example, if your stove stops working and they can't find the part to repair it, the home warranty company will replace the entire stove for free. If you need something repaired, all you need to do is call to make an appointment for a technician to come over. Make sure you are there when the technician arrives to fix the item, pay the technician for the nominal service fee, and then you are done. It is that simple.

## Changing Your Bills' Due Date

Most bills are due on different days of the month, do you agree? Most of us will. With this, our minds cannot be settled knowing that one of the bills will be due soon. My suggestion is to call all your creditors and request that they change all your due dates to the day that is convenient for you. Once this task is completed and you can pay all your bills on one day, this will not only save you tons of time, but it will illuminate late fees. So, get on those calls and make the change.

## STORY TIME

I always try to live a simple life. So much that my business is called Simply Shiral, my website is *www.simplyshiral.com*, my email address is *shiral@simplyshiral.com*, the titles of all my workshops end with "Made Simple," and

this book is entitled *Rental Properties Made Simple*. In theory, if I keep things simple, I will have more time to learn and do all the wonderful things I want to do.

But because I own two small businesses, manage many rental properties, do my own bookkeeping, plus much more, I sometimes become overwhelmed. My friend, Carol Pilkington, who is a spiritual counselor (*www.carolpilkington.com*) says, "Stay in the present moment." I learned from her that no matter how many things take up space in my mind, I need to remember to "stay in the present moment." When I do this, I become focused on the one thing that I am doing and find myself calmer and able to get the task completed. This has been life-changing for me and is truly the root of all simplicity. So to all you readers, take Carol's advice and "stay in the present moment."

Simplifying your business leaves time for you to enjoy it. I love the many things I do, but I would not have the time and energy to do all of it if I didn't simplify.

As Robin S. Sharma (speaker and author of *The Monk Who Sold His Ferrari*) says, "Never overlook the power of simplicity."

## Summary

1. Use a calendar to keep track of your daily activities and your upcoming repairs and the maintenance of your building.

2. Make copies of all your forms and documents for easy access.

3. Consider purchasing a home warranty service.

4. Consider changing all your sporadic due dates for your bills to one day in the month.

# Conclusion

I hope I taught you some things you didn't know, answered some questions you had, and most of all, inspired you to take on your property investment journey with confidence. If you are still feeling overwhelmed and want to learn more, please visit my website at *www.simplyshiral.com* to see a list of my simple, low-cost workshops that include all the property management topics I discuss in this book.

If you would like to book a free thirty-minute one-on-one phone session with me (yes, with me), please contact me at *shiral@ simplyshiral.com*. Helping you, my reader, become successful is my way of thanking you for taking the time to read my book. I am most grateful to you! I wish you all the luck in your future rental property and investment business ventures.

Now, if I may, I'd like to leave you with one last story.

## STORY TIME

My husband and I were in our early thirties when we purchased our first house. It was a single-family home. If I had the knowledge that I have today back when we were in our twenties, I would have purchased a four-plex, lived in one of the units and rented out the others. I would have paid the mortgage and property expenses with the rents collected from the three rented units. I

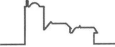
would pretend that we were paying rent and deposited it into a separate account that we would not touch. I would then continue to save until we had enough for a down payment on a single-family home for our family.

Once we were able to purchase a single-family home, I would rent out the unit in the fourplex we had lived in, and then that rental income would pay the mortgage on our new single-family home. With this strategy, we would have been able to buy our home sooner than we did. Since I didn't have this knowledge in my twenties, I am passing it on to you now, hoping that you can either use this strategy or brainstorm different options that will fit your lifestyle.

I have learned throughout my journey that most people stick with the status quo. Because of the cards I was dealt, I needed to live outside of the box to even have a chance of succeeding. So I did what I thought was best for my family and me regardless of what society expected me to do. People have told me that real estate investing is risky. I say many things in life are risky and real estate investing is one of the best things Jaime and I ever did for ourselves and our family.

What will you do for yours?

Much aloha,

*Shiral*

# Acknowledgments

I would like to thank my daughter, Anita. Neen, your presence in the world, since I gave birth to you when I was sixteen years old, inspires me to do my very best. I am always in awe of you, especially when I think about all you have achieved and continue to achieve. Your brilliance and integrity inspires me every day of my life and I love you with all my heart.

I would also like to thank my son, Jaime. Jaim, you have the kindest soul of anyone I have ever met and everyone who enters your world is lucky to be in it. I am so honored to be one of them. I truly believe you have been here before and I am so grateful to have you as my son. Your integrity along with your kindness is always an inspiration to me. I love you with all my heart.

To my parents, Ralph and Shirley Pereira, who have passed on but are still guiding me. I thank you for instilling in me the values, morals, and integrity that I live by, and also for always believing in me. I love and miss you both dearly.

I would like to thank my four very special friends who I love with all my heart; Kristy, for your ongoing unconditional love and support since the very special day I met you in 1988. You are the definition of a true friend. Jocella, for our very special friendship filled with honesty and trust. Your style of always keeping it real helps me improve myself no matter how hard it may sometimes be. Muriel, for inviting me over for lunch and making my favorite

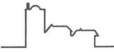 

meal, and not taking no for an answer when I say *I can't come over because I am working.* Your motherly ways of reminding me the importance of taking a break are appreciated. And Leslie, my dear friend and colleague. You are my daily inspiration. Without having you to talk to, my business would not be where it is today. It has and continues to be an honor and a pleasure to work and grow with you. All I can say is…watch out world, here comes the ladies!

And Jerry Craig, I would have never thought I would meet a great friend on my early morning walk when the rest of the city is sleeping except for you and me. I appreciate your wisdom, kindness, and all the wonderful tips you gave me as I developed this book. I look forward to seeing you every morning on my walk and I am grateful to have you as my friend.

My Pereira and Torres/Sanchez families, your constant love and support has always given me the drive to reach the goals I set out for myself.

Stacy, Stacy, Stacy Dymalski, (*www.thememoirmidwife.com*) if I didn't meet you on April 30, 2017, at the Ultimate Women's Expo, I would not have been inspired to take that leap to turn my story into a book. With you in my life now, nothing is impossible.

And last, to you, Jaime, my husband, best friend, soul mate, and my number one fan. I thank you from the bottom of my heart for all your support and not questioning any new idea I come up with especially when the idea seems unreachable, for always making sure the water in the tea kettle is hot so I have an endless pot of tea, and most of all, for all your massages when my neck is killing me. I love you more than the air I breathe.

# About the Author

Truly a self-made woman, Shiral grew up in the "hood" of Los Angeles, getting good grades, playing sports after school, and running from gang members who came from outside the neighborhood in which she lived. Shiral had her first child at sixteen years old with her high school sweetheart. She and her baby's father eventually wed, had another child, and they are still a happy couple today. After giving birth, Shiral continued her education until she graduated from California State University, Los Angeles, with a BA degree in Sociology that included an emphasis in alcohol and substance abuse addiction. Afterward, she landed a job in South Los Angeles as a drug counselor where she worked for many years and became known for a Parenting Skills class she developed and still teaches.

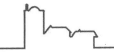
On her two-hour round trip commute to work, Shiral listened to real estate tapes and memorized the lessons and content each one had to offer. One day she had a thought about investing in real estate, and the next thing she knew she and her husband bought a four-plex, which was the beginning of a family business. Continuing to purchase properties across the United States, Shiral learned every aspect of buying, selling, renting, and managing property so well that she unexpectedly became the go-to person when anyone she knew needed advice about being a landlord. Which is what led her to writing this book and developing her popular classes on real estate investment, finance management, and property management.

A life skills coach, Shiral also teaches workshops on caregiving and parenting, and is an active volunteer for the Alzheimer's Association. Her passions include raising funds for the National Alliance on Mental Illness, continuous self-improvement, and living a simple lifestyle. Her philosophy on simple living is due to her passion for the environment…less is more. Shiral is the proud mom of two adult children and lives in Burbank, California, with her husband of thirty-three years. You may reach her through her website at *www.SimplyShiral.com.*

Made in the USA
Middletown, DE
28 March 2019